LOVELY PEGGY

LOVELY PEGGY

A PLAY IN THREE ACTS BASED ON
THE LOVE ROMANCE OF MARGARET
WOFFINGTON AND DAVID GARRICK

BY

J. R. CRAWFORD

NEW HAVEN:
YALE UNIVERSITY PRESS
MCMXI

Copyright, 1911
BY
YALE UNIVERSITY PRESS

Printed from type. 750 copies. May, 1911.

Dramatic and all other rights reserved

PRINTED IN THE UNITED STATES

PUBLISHER'S NOTE

The play following was submitted in a competition held by the Yale University Dramatic Association, 1910-1911, although it was ineligible for any prize award because of the fact that the author was a member of the University faculty. It is now, in response to many requests, published in book form through the co-operation of the Yale University Dramatic Association and of certain graduates of the University.

LOVELY PEGGY

THE SCENES

Act I. The Green Room, Covent Garden Theatre, October, 1741.

Act II. The House in Southampton Street, November, 1742.

Act III. The Stage of Covent Garden Theatre, some months later.

CAST OF CHARACTERS

Peg Woffington, leading actress of Covent Garden Theatre.

David Garrick, a wine-merchant, and afterwards actor manager of Drury Lane Theatre.

Sir Charles Hanbury Williams, a man of fashion.

John Rich, manager of Covent Garden Theatre.

James Quin, an actor of the old school.

Charles Macklin, an actor and friend of Garrick.

Tate Wilkinson, an applicant for a position on the stage.

George Anne Bellamy, of Covent Garden Theatre.

Dr. Samuel Johnson.

Pompey, servant to Mrs. Woffington.

Hodgson, Garrick's butler.

A Servant at Covent Garden.

A Scene-shifter.

First Gallant.

Second Gallant.

Third Gallant.

A Call-boy.

Gallants, men of fashion, members of the audience, stage hands, etc.

LOVELY PEGGY

ACT I

SCENE: *The Green Room at Covent Garden Theatre, October, 1741. A large room, rather plainly furnished. There are three doors, two on the right and one on the left. Center, a fireplace and over it a portrait of Betterton. A bust of Shakespeare, a large oak cabinet, a plain table and a few chairs complete the furnishings. The room is lighted by candles. It is the night of a performance of Farquhar's "Constant Couple," in which Peg Woffington is playing the part of Sir Harry Wildair. Discovered: James Quin, a portly actor of the old school, and Miss George Anne Bellamy. Quin is a gruff, surly man, thickset and heavy, inclined to be taciturn but with sudden flashes of "Saturnine humor." George Anne Bellamy is a beautiful young actress with blue child-like eyes and golden hair. She is vain, self-conscious and affected. The adoration and flattery which her beauty has always met with has made her a spoiled child. Quin is pacing angrily up and down the room while Miss Bellamy is trying the effect of various feathers and trinkets in her hair. She poses continually before a large mirror.*

LOVELY PEGGY

Quin

And I tell you again the town is mad! They have no eyes for me when Peg Woffington is on the stage! No more applause for James Quin than if I were a puppet!

Bellamy

Her impertinence amuses the vulgar taste.

Quin

Why, hark'ee, Mrs. Bellamy,—I knew Peg Woffington when she peddled oranges in the streets of Dublin—aye, and went barefoot, too! Now, egad, not content with acting like a woman, she must needs act like a man! Sir Harry Wildair! What can an Irish orange wench know about acting Sir Harry Wildair?

Bellamy

It's vastly indelicate to wear breeches and play men's parts.

Quin

The impudent Irish-faced hussy! Ah, Mrs. Bellamy, you should have seen Wilks play Sir Harry. There was a man! None of your damned mincing gait and squeaking pipe when he played it!

Bellamy

[*Yawning.*]
It must have been prodigious.—Er, Mr. Quin?

LOVELY PEGGY

Quin

Well? What is it? What is it?

Bellamy

Who was the handsome young gallant in the wings who tried to seize me as I came off tonight?

Quin

Bah! D'ye think I've nothing better to do than note every coxcomb that smirks in a woman's face?

Bellamy

Dear Mr. Quin! He said that your acting was the marvel of the age.

Quin

He did, eh? Pooh—there are no critics left—they are all dead. In my day—

Bellamy

And he praised your grand pause.

Quin

Come, he's a young fellow of taste. Could it be Sir Charles?

Bellamy

Sir Charles?

Quin

Aye, Sir Charles Hanbury Williams—the wit and man of fashion he calls himself. He is dangling after Woffington and has been these six months.

Bellamy

Dangling after the Woffington woman—oh!

Quin

What did he say about my grand pause? Some clever epigram, I warrant you.

Bellamy

Oh, nothing.

Quin

What! Nothing! Why, you said—

Bellamy

I know—it was of no moment.

Quin

Madam, I tell you it was of the greatest possible moment. The approbation of Sir Charles carries with it the approval of the Town. What he says today—the Bedford Coffee House thinks tomorrow!

Bellamy

I'll endeavor to recollect what it was. I know—your pause was marked by a dignity of bearing that—er—er—

Quin

Pray continue, Madam.

LOVELY PEGGY

Bellamy

That imparted majesty to the scene. It was something like that.

Quin

I shall treasure those words. Only two weeks ago I knocked the prompter down, madam, for interrupting my grand pause.

Bellamy
Oh!

Quin

Yes, madam, knocked him down. When I came to the great scene of the play—I paused to permit the effect to sink in. Then what does this confounded puppy of a prompter do, but commence bellowing my lines to me from the wings. I paid no attention at first.

Bellamy
Of course not.

Quin

Finally, madam, he fairly shouted at me and some jackanapes in the pit laughed. I strode up to him and knocked him down and then returned and finished the scene—after apologizing to the pit for the interruption.

Bellamy
Serve him right.

LOVELY PEGGY

Quin

But what do these puppets know of acting today? In my day we understood the dignity that goes with such an art.

[*Going up to Bellamy and taking her chin in his hand.*]

You are young, child, and have a pretty face—don't let that spoil you as it has the Woffington woman. Learn to be an actress. It's worth more than the poems the fine gentlemen in the boxes write you.

[*Enter John Rich, the manager, carrying a cat. He is dressed shabbily and has a coarse face. His accent is that of an uneducated man.*]

Rich

There y'are. Two hundred pounds in the house tonight,—it's the Woffington woman draws the town. And I larned her to act myself.

Quin

Acting! Do you suppose it's acting the town comes to see? A pretty woman is all they want. Do they come to see me any more—me, James Quin? I can act as Betterton acted and there's not another man alive today can say that. And they laughed at my grand pause!

LOVELY PEGGY

Rich

You lack distinction, Muster Quin. You should imitate my Richard III.

Quin

Bah!

Bellamy

I am convinced, Mr. Rich, that if you would display your talents once more before the town, we should all be censured for our shortcomings. Compared to you, our acting must seem presumptuous.

Rich

Mrs. Bellamy—you're a prodigious fine woman, and, egad, for a female, you've good taste.

[*She curtsies to the ground with great formality and Rich attempts a clumsy bow in return.*]

Quin

Pish! The minx is only laughing at you, Rich.

Bellamy

Nay, I protest!

Rich

[*His face changes—suspiciously.*]

I'll larn you to laugh at me, you French doll,—or you too, Quin.

Bellamy

I vow, Mr. Rich, that I spoke in earnest.

Rich

Well,—well.

[*Enter a servant from the door R.*]

Servant

[*To Rich.*]
A young man to see you, sir.

Rich

To see me? Tell him to go to the devil!

Servant

Yes, sir.

Rich

Another scribbler—eh!

Servant

He did not state his business, sir.

Rich

[*To Quin.*]
I'll warrant you it's a playwright,—curse 'em!

Quin

And I'll wager it's a young spark to carry off Mrs. Bellamy here!

Rich

[*To the servant.*]
What's his name? Eh?

LOVELY PEGGY

Servant
Garrick, sir—David Garrick.

Rich
[*Laughs.*]
Egad—it's the little wine-merchant!

Quin
Aye, I hear he's turned strolling player—he's been at Ipswich this summer—'faith, Rich, when the wine-merchants turn players,—there's naught left for us poor players to do but drink ourselves to death!

Rich
[*To the servant.*]
Tell Muster David Garrick I'm not wanting any port today. Eh, Quin?
[*Rich laughs uproariously as the servant bows and goes out.*]

Quin
The fool was sitting in the stage-box again tonight. He's another fly buzzing after Woffington.

Bellamy
But his eyes! Have you marked Mr. Garrick's eyes? They are like fire!

Rich
You have marked his eyes, have you, eh? What the devil have his eyes got to do with you?

Quin

[*Chuckles.*]

That's the woman! 'Cod, to think they note the eyes of every mortal in the pit!

Bellamy

[*Angry.*]

Mr. Garrick has sat every night in the same box since the season opened. Is it so strange that I have seen him?

Quin

No, but it is that he has not seen you! His eyes, I hear, are all for Mrs. Woffington.

[*Bellamy tosses her head.*]

Aye, you may quarrel for him between you,— he's a fine catch, what with his three quarts of vinegar and calling himself a wine-merchant, and his strolling acting. Much good will you get of him.

Bellamy

Brute! You judge women's minds, Mr. Quin, by your own.

Quin

Aye, and it has not led me into many errors, either.

[*The servant re-enters from the right, and comes forward.*]

LOVELY PEGGY

Servant.

Mr. David Garrick, sir, presents his compliments and begs that you will grant him a brief interview. He wishes to become a member of the company at Covent Garden.

Rich

He does, eh? Then let him larn to act. Covent Garden Theatre has no need for wine-merchants or strolling players. Tell him to go home and drown himself in his own tun of wine.
[*Laughs boisterously. The servant bows and goes out of the door R.*]

Rich

What would become of my theatre if I wasted my time on every coxcomb who thought he could act? Egad, 'tis trouble enough with those I have without adding to my stock. Eh?
[*Enter the call-boy from the door L.*]

Call-boy

Mr. Quin! First call for the epilogue.

Quin

[*Going towards door.*]
Anon! Must you make such a devil's own row? Do you think I am deaf?

LOVELY PEGGY

[*Goes out with call-boy, pinching the latter's ear.*]

Bellamy

Dear Mr. Rich! Are you going to give me a nice part in the new play? A very nice part?

Rich

Aye, 'twill be good enough, I daresay.

Bellamy

Good enough! Why, that's not half good enough! I want a very big part,—dear Mr. Rich,—and you shall teach me how to act it as it should be acted!

Rich

Girl, you're laughing at me!

Bellamy

[*With extreme affection.*]
No, I am not, dear Mr. Rich. Would you accuse me of wearing the hypocrite's mask?

Rich

I am not a man to be wheedled by a pretty face.

Bellamy

But surely you must be sensible that, if I *have* a pretty face, as you say, the public will prefer it to one growing a little—shall we say—faded?

Rich

Woffington has only been here a year,—she has only begun to profit by my lessons.

Bellamy

True. But does she ever allow you to be the cause of whatever merit she may possess? Does she show her gratitude to one who has been almost more than a father to her?

Rich

Aye, there's something in that. I heard them say at the Bedford Coffee House that Mrs. Woffington called me the Harlequin of cats—

Bellamy

There's gratitude for you! I've heard—but I won't talk scandalous gossip!

Rich

What is it you heard?

Bellamy

Nay, I protest! I fear it would give offence—

Rich

You must tell me, madam! I won't submit to this plotting and scheming behind my back. I took that Irish wench out of a Dublin gutter and larned her to act and gave her nine pound a week to boot—and now she turns on me, sharper than a thankless tooth.

Bellamy

I dreaded to make you angry by repeating it. But as there is nothing so base as ingratitude, so there should be no hesitation in laying it bare. Mrs. Woffington said that you were—please, I dare not say it—

Rich

[*Clenching his fists.*]
Go on, Mrs. Bellamy! I am a philosopher!

Bellamy

[*With concealed maliciousness.*]
Woffington called you an ignorant old fool!

Rich

[*His voice trembling with rage.*]
Mrs. Bellamy, you shall have as big a part as you could wish.

Bellamy

[*Curtseying.*]
I am deeply in your debt—nor will you find me lacking in appreciation.

Rich

You shall play Monimia in The Orphan—damme, I'll buy you a new dress for it—anything you want—we'll show the town and that Woffington woman there's some merit in you, Mrs. Bellamy.

LOVELY PEGGY

Bellamy

Your kindness overwhelms me! But I had hoped for some new part—The Orphan is a stock piece and will not draw the town at first —as a novelty would.

Rich

[*Goes to a large cupboard, which he opens. Several dozen manuscripts, of all shapes and sizes, tumble on to the floor as he opens the door.*]

Here y'are—there's drama for you!

[*Points to the mass of manuscripts.*]

Bellamy

What is that strange mountain of paper?

Rich

Plays—all of 'em—unacted plays—tragedies— comedies—operas—some of 'em have been there for years.

Bellamy

Heavens! Have you read all those plays?

Rich

I never read plays. Never read one in my life. But every poet and scribbler in town sends 'em in. I only play what the fashionable people want. It's their money runs this theatre. Do these damned scribblers ever risk their money? Not they—they haven't any. It's men like Sir Charles Williams that tell me what to play. It's their cash. But hark'ee, Mrs. Bellamy—I'd like to do ye a favor. If you can find a part there that suits ye, I'll put it on, damme if I don't!

[*Mrs. Bellamy, with a little cry of delight, runs across the stage, and sits on the floor as she turns over the pile of manuscripts. Enter, at this point, from the door R., Sir Charles Hanbury Williams, a tall, handsome man, with signs of dissipation in his face. His movements are languid but graceful. He steps rather deliberately and scrutinizes Bellamy through his eyeglass as he advances.*]

Rich

[*Bowing obsequiously.*]

Good evening, Sir Charles!

Sir Charles

Confound you, Rich—take your litter of cats away!

[*To Bellamy.*]

Ah—Mrs. Bellamy—what a charming picture! Beauty choosing between comedy and tragedy. A worthy crown for each.

[*He bows and takes snuff.*]

LOVELY PEGGY

Bellamy

[*Rising and curtseying.*]
Flattery in a wit, Sir Charles! Fie!

Sir Charles

Flattery to you would be impossible, even were I capable of such a vice. Where beauty and art are so much in harmony—the truth proclaims itself.

[*Turns to Rich.*]
Our lovely Peggy is getting her accustomed applause tonight—I hear. Her Sir Harry Wildair has brought us in a tidy little sum, eh, Rich?

Rich

Two hundred pounds in the house tonight, Sir Charles.

Sir Charles

Ah—then we may announce it for the following week, may we not?

Rich

Why, sir, as for that—

Sir Charles

Come, come! I have promised Peggy. You would not have me break my promise to a lovely woman? Announce Mrs. Woffington in Sir Harry Wildair for next week, d'ye hear?

Rich

Yes, Sir Charles.

Sir Charles

By the bye, Rich,—my lawyer has brought the sum you mentioned,—ahem! He's ready to attend you.

Rich

The money for the new play? One thousand pounds—

Sir Charles

Yes, yes—the sum does not matter. Arrange that at your convenience.

Rich

I'll go to him straightway.

Sir Charles

Pray, do so, by all means.

[*Exit Rich through the door R.*]

Sir Charles

[*To Mrs. Bellamy.*]

Mrs. Bellamy, I have long sought this opportunity to assure you of my devotion to your genius.

Bellamy

Your approbation, Sir Charles, is an honor, knowing as I do the excellence of your critical taste.

LOVELY PEGGY

Sir Charles

[*Coughs slightly as he flicks some snuff off a ruffle.*]

My critical taste, madam, as you are pleased to call it, is ever at the service of a beautiful woman.

Bellamy

Then I wonder, Sir Charles, if you would do a favor for me?

Sir Charles

[*Looks at her sharply and comes a step nearer.*]

Any commands with which Mrs. Bellamy may honor me, I shall obey to the very letter.

Bellamy

You spoke to Mr. Rich about—about Mrs. Woffington?

Sir Charles

There's the rub, is it? And what have you to say about Mrs. Woffington?

Bellamy

Will you persuade Mr. Rich to let me have a part suited to my talents? Will you have him announce me in some new play?

Sir Charles

Can you draw the town, madam, like our lovely Peggy?

Bellamy

I am as pretty as she is! And I can act—I know it—I feel it! What chance have I had in small parts—with Mrs. Woffington taking all the applause! All I wish is an opportunity.

Sir Charles

And if you fail, madam, have you ever thought of that? Do you realize what it means to face the hisses of an angry audience? They spoil their favorites—but are without pity for those who fail to please.

Bellamy

I am prepared for that! They shall listen to me as they do to Peg Woffington!

Sir Charles

And if I grant you this favor, Mrs. Bellamy?

Bellamy

Sir, I will be your grateful servant—I'll do anything for you!

Sir Charles

Anything! child—remember—when I grant my favors to the fair sex, I only grant them on

LOVELY PEGGY

condition. Do not let us misunderstand one another. Are you prepared to pay a fair *quid pro quo*?

[*Coming close to her.*]

Bellamy

[*Shrinks back, then nerves herself.*]
Yes.

Sir Charles

[*He looks at her steadily, then bows over her hand, which he kisses.*]

You shall have the next new play, madam, I'll see Rich tonight—and—er—I'll pacify the Woffington—I have a—certain—influence in that quarter. My chaise will call for you tomorrow—there is a charming little house and garden of which I am the owner—but it shall be wholly at your disposition.

[*As he again takes her hand and presses it fervently to his lips, Peg Woffington enters from the door R. She is dressed as Sir Harry Wildair, in white satin, closely fitting breeches, white silk stockings and black pumps, with red heels. Her coat is also of white satin trimmed with silver brocade. On her head she wears a small man's wig, but no hat. At her side hangs a light court sword. As she sees Sir Charles kiss Bellamy's hand, she dashes angrily forward, drawing her stage sword in her fury, and lunges at Sir Charles. He turns quickly, and coolly, with a deft motion, catches Peg's wrist and presses it. As he does so, she drops the sword with a cry of pain. He puts his foot on the sword, releases her wrist and bows with extreme formal politeness.*]

Sir Charles

[*With ironical sarcasm.*]

You are behind the scenes now, my lovely Peggy,—and Sir Harry Wildair is but a woman after all.

Peg

[*Panting with rage.*]

How dare you to presume to touch me!

Sir Charles

[*Picking up her sword.*]

To prevent you from doing a mischief with this stage bauble.

[*Tests the blade, smiling, and bends it.*]

A pretty thing,—but, like a woman, a dangerous toy for the unskilled.

Bellamy

[*Comes forward.*]

It may please you to know, Mrs. Woffington,

that Sir Charles has promised *me* the next new play.

Peg

Never! I forbid it! Do you hear? Never! Never! Never!

Bellamy

[*Laughs.*]

You forbid it? And pray by what authority?

Peg

By my own! I'll see Mr. Rich myself—I'll have you turned out of the theatre!

Sir Charles

Can it be that lovely Peggy is jealous?

Peg

Not of this doll! A silly, simpering French milliner!

Bellamy

At least you will allow that my voice doesn't squeak!

Sir Charles

[*Sits on table, thoroughly enjoying the quarrel.*]

Aye, Peg! She had you there!

LOVELY PEGGY

Peg

Her voice lacks all expression whatever! It is like the mechanical bird in Cox's Museum.

Bellamy

My art is womanly. *I* do not need to strut about in breeches and ape the men.

Peg

Aye, we know well enough that you do not dare to show the truth about your figure!

Sir Charles

Egad, Peggy, you've settled for the squeaking voice! Eh, Bellamy?

Bellamy

Je m'en fiche! One cannot expect manners from an orange woman!

Peg

Nor virtue in the French!

Sir Charles

Nor love and charity on the stage,—you might add! Life is—

Peg

I don't care a farthing rush for life, or your sentiments on this subject!

LOVELY PEGGY

Bellamy

Nor did the man who mimicked your voice from a box last night care for yours!

Peg

Tate Wilkinson! A beggar—a hanger on of the theatre—who thinks because he can mimic others that he can act himself. He dared to mock me last night—but he shall pay for it! If he has the audacity to present himself here again—I'll show you whether Peg Woffington has any influence in this theatre!

Sir Charles

Tate Wilkinson is a clever boy. I am thinking of recommending him for a position here. He keeps the Bedford in a roar with his mimicry. It was a bold thing to do, Peg, to mock you to your face. I like his spirit.

Peg

I hope he will like mine! The mean, pitiful hound—

Sir Charles

Ah, Peggy, you do not hate as prettily as you love!

Peg

[*Comes close to him.*]
Do you dare to speak that word to me—now?

LOVELY PEGGY

Sir Charles

Caution would best become you, madam! There are eager ears listening.

Peg

Perhaps you prefer to listen to this pert creature?
[*Nods insultingly at Bellamy.*]

Sir Charles
[*Coolly.*]
And if I do? Strong diet may pall.

Peg

[*Stamps her foot in a frenzy of rage.*]
You brute! You shameless libertine! You rake!
[*Sir Charles laughs heartily at this and slaps his knee.*]

Sir Charles

You never acted better in your life, Peggy!

Peg

[*Beside herself with jealous rage—rushes at Bellamy.*]
As for you!
[*Seizes Bellamy by the shoulders and shakes her violently. Bellamy screams. They struggle a moment, while Williams is un-*

LOVELY PEGGY

able to control his laughter. Peg's short wig comes off, and her hair tumbles down over her shoulders. Bellamy slips out of her grasp, and runs screaming from the room. Sir Charles stoops, picks up Peg's wig, and hands it to her with a bow.]

Sir Charles

No gentleman should be seen without his wig!
[*Peg snatches it from him and begins to bind up her hair, panting with rage.*]

Peg

Understand me, Sir Charles, after your conduct tonight there can be nothing further between us. I am done!

Sir Charles

Surely, you are not jealous of Bellamy? Have I ever reproached you with the young spark in the stage-box—at whom I've seen you cast glances more than once. Pray, permit me the same indulgence.

Peg

I have never spoken to Mr. David Garrick in my life.

Sir Charles

But you know his name. Perhaps you have seen a poem in the Gentleman's Magazine—to "Sylvia," by D. G.?

LOVELY PEGGY

Peg

And if I have? Am I to be blamed for every fop that writes me verses?

Sir Charles

Ah, he wrote them to you? I was only aware that they appeared in a newspaper.

Peg

[*Bites her lip with vexation.*]
This continual suspicion is intolerable.

Sir Charles

Because you have given me continual cause.

Peg

Then I intend no longer to grant you the right to question my actions.

Sir Charles

Agreed! I long ago ceased to look for either gratitude or appreciation from you, madam.

Peg

Nor did I expect gentlemanly behavior from you. We are quits, at all events.

Sir Charles

Aye, quits, as you call it, Peggy! For the present—

LOVELY PEGGY

Peg

[Taking a trinket from her dress.]

There!

[Throws it at his feet.]

Sir Charles

Behold the tragedy queen! You are much better in comedy, Peggy.

[Enter a servant, followed by Tate Wilkinson, a poor and needy young man, who is making a vain search for a position as an actor.]

Servant

Mr. Tate Wilkinson desires to wait here to see Mr. Rich, if you please.

Wilkinson

[Comes forward—to Peg who has turned her back.]

If you have any pity—help me to get an interview with him. I can act—but I am starving—

Sir Charles

Come now, Peggy, what do you say? Here is a fellow-actor implores your pity.

Peg

[Turns around, her eyes flashing, and goes up to Wilkinson.]

LOVELY PEGGY

Mr. Wilkinson, your impudence to me last night is proof of your ignorance. When you mimicked me in public, I commanded Mr. Rich not to give you any engagement whatever, not even of the most menial kind. You deserve neither charity nor pity, or my purse would have given you a dinner. I sincerely hope, in whatever barn you are suffered as an unworthy stroller, that you will fully experience the same contempt you dared last night to offer me.

[*With a flounce she turns from him and goes up stage, leaving Wilkinson crushed and dejected.*]

Sir Charles

Do you still desire to see Mr. Rich?

Wilkinson

No. I—I—. Ah, well, I will go.

[*Seeing that his case is hopeless, he walks slowly and sorrowfully away and goes out the door R., followed by the servant.*]

Sir Charles

Your reputation for charity, madam, will suffer, I fear.

Peg

I would have forgiven him anything but an insult upon the stage. Let him mimic me in

LOVELY PEGGY

hole-and-corner coffee-houses if he chooses—but not when I am playing at Covent Garden.

[*Enter, after a noise of talking and laughter off-stage, Quin, Macklin and Rich. Macklin is a portly man with a strongly lined face.*]

Quin

[*To Peg, bowing.*]

I wondered, when I heard the applause tonight, madam, whether the town admired more your art or your beauty?

Peg

The applause, which you confess to hearing, answered your question, sir, sufficiently.

Sir Charles

Have a care, Quin! The lady is not to be trifled with.

Macklin

Madam, your servant!

[*Bows and kisses her hand. Turns to Quin.*]

Mr. Quin, because we aim today to hold the mirror up to nature, you should not censure acting which differs from the school with which you are familiar.

Rich

Macklin, you speak too damned familiarly on the stage. I don't like it.

LOVELY PEGGY

Quin

[*To Macklin.*]

Sir, you may remember that I said your last comedy would be damned?

Macklin

Well, sir?

Quin

[*Chuckling.*]

It was damned,—the public would none of it.

Macklin

Well, sir?

Quin

What do you think of my judgment in matters of the stage now?

Macklin

Why, I think posterity will do me justice.

Quin

I believe they will, sir, for now it's only your play that is damned; but posterity will have the satisfaction to know that both play and actor met the same fate!

Peg

A truce—a truce. I am weary of all your pompous squabbles about plays and acting. I never bother my head about either,—and yet, by the applause I received this evening, I verily think half the town believes me to be a real man.

Quin

Madam, the other half knows you to be a woman!

[*Peg walks away in some confusion, while the others, even Macklin, roar.*]

Sir Charles

Egad, Quin, you've performed a miracle! I wager you made the Irish girl blush!

[*Enter a servant from the door R.*]

Servant

[*To Rich.*]

The young wine-merchant to see you, sir,—Mr. David Garrick.

Rich

I'm busy—it's inconvenient. What the devil! I've sent him away twice tonight!

Servant

He instructed me to say,—begging your pardon, sir, that he intended to return until you did see him.

Rich

The confounded impudent puppy!

LOVELY PEGGY

[*To the servant.*]
You blockhead! How dare you bring me such a message?

Peg

[*Comes forward. To the servant.*]
Show Mr. Garrick in, please. Mr. Rich will see him.

Rich

Zounds!—what—what's this? Do nothing of the kind!

Sir Charles

Do you hear? Send him packing!

Peg

[*To the servant.*]
You heard me. Show Mr. Garrick in!

Servant

Yes, madam.

[*Bows and retires hastily.*]

Rich

[*To Peg.*]
Would you defy me, madam, in my own theatre?

Sir Charles

Aye,—she would defy the devil in his,—and I've no doubt he owns one.

LOVELY PEGGY

Peg

Mr. Garrick is a young man of parts—and by reports from Ipswich where he lately played, will be a great actor.

Quin

Aye, he's been ogling you from the boxes,—'tis all he needs to teach him to act.

Sir Charles

It is the neat little man who sits in the right hand stage-box? I know him, a low fellow—and a tradesman.

Macklin

Well, sir, and what if he were a tradesman?

Sir Charles

Oh, nothing, I assure you,—'tis all one to me.
[*To Peg.*]
Madam, permit me to congratulate you upon— shall we say—your most recent admirer? Egad, if we could all escape our wine-bills so easily!

[*Enter the servant from the door R.*]

Servant

[*Announcing.*]
Mr. David Garrick!

[*Enter David Garrick, a small, nervous, fussy man, with a diffident manner and a hesitat-*

LOVELY PEGGY

ing trick of speech. *His clothes are neat and he obviously gives much attention to his dress, as far as his rather limited means will permit.*]

Garrick

[*Bows.*]
Madam—your servant! Mr. Rich, sir, I—I—I—

Rich

Don't eye me, sir!

Garrick

If I might make so bold, by your leave, sir—

Sir Charles

Pay your wine-bill, Rich, and send him away.

Garrick

I was not—not aware, sir, that I was addressing you?

Sir Charles

No? Do you see any offence in my conduct, sir?

Garrick

This is not the place to—to answer that question.

Sir Charles

I would have you know, sir, that I am not accustomed to pick and choose where or how I talk to tradesmen.

LOVELY PEGGY

Peg

[*Stepping between them.*]

Mr. Garrick is my friend,—and it is my wish that he be received accordingly.

Sir Charles

Pardon me, madam, I understood the young man was unknown to you—except—ah, of course—I was forgetting the stage-box and the poetry! [*To Garrick.*]

You are a critic, as well, I believe? A most accomplished person, truly! Did you find the barns at Ipswich very draughty, sir?

Peg

If you persist in your insults, Sir Charles, Mr. Garrick may forget that he is a gentleman.

Sir Charles

Wine-merchants have short memories and long accounts. Pray, let the young man speak for himself, madam.

Garrick.

My business for the moment is with Mr. Rich.

Peg

Mr. Rich will grant you an interview.

Sir Charles

The Woffington is in command, Rich. Let us

withdraw and not interrupt so charming a *tête-à-tête*.

Rich

[*Snarls.*]
I can't talk to him. I'm busy!

Garrick

Nevertheless, madam, I thank you for your courtesy.
[*Bows.*]

Peg

Theatrical managers delight in making simple matters difficult. I was myself compelled to call upon Mr. Rich nineteen times before he would receive me. And yet, but for me, the season would have been a failure. Theatrical managers, Mr. Garrick, cannot see an inch beyond their noses, although their business is further off.

Rich

Well, well, what is it you want, Muster Garrick, eh? Come, come, sir,—don't keep me waiting.

Garrick

I have called to apply for a position in the theatrical company at Covent Garden.

Rich

Want to act, eh? Ever done any acting, eh?

LOVELY PEGGY

Garrick

This summer, sir, at Ipswich—I played a few small parts—not without success.

Rich

What were they, eh?

Garrick

Aboan in Oroonoko—and a few others. The season was a brief one.

Rich

[*With scorn.*]

A strolling actor, eh? And what do you think, sir, a strolling actor could do at Covent Garden? This is the temple of the Muses, sir!

Quin

[*To Garrick.*]

Neither your presence, sir, nor your personality possesses that dignity or decorum which is one of the first requisites for an actor. There, sir, on that wall is a portrait of Betterton. Look on that picture, sir, and then on this!

[*Points to Garrick's image in the mirror.*]

Garrick

[*Quietly.*]

I did not come here, Mr. Quin, to receive a lesson in acting, but to give one.

LOVELY PEGGY

Quin

What! Why, you—you—

Peg

I think I can vouch for the truth of Mr. Garrick's statement. If the reports from Ipswich may be trusted—coupled with a private exhibition of Mr. Garrick's which I once saw without his knowledge—

Sir Charles

Private exhibition? Aye, I warrant the truth of the last, Rich!

[*Slaps Rich on the back heavily to the latter's obvious displeasure.*]

Peg

[*With dignity.*]

If you have exhausted your pleasantry, Sir Charles, Mr. Garrick will favor us with a recitation.

Sir Charles

Oh, by all means! A recitation is the thing! Damme, let's hear the wine-merchant decant his claret!

Macklin

Sir, I think you will allow that I am an actor not entirely without judgment?

Sir Charles

I've always said, my boy, that it was a pity a clever fellow like you should be a player.

Macklin

What would you have me be, Sir Charles, a baronet?

Sir Charles

Confound your impudence!

Macklin

As I was on the point of observing, I would like to add my opinion in Mr. Garrick's favor, to that of Mrs. Woffington. What will you recite, Mr. Garrick? A passage from Richard the Third?

Rich

No—that's my part. I will not suffer a bungler to repeat my best part.

Garrick

There is a scene in Alexander the Great, or the Rival Queens, which I had thought would display my talents.

Quin

Alexander the Little, I believe you to mean, sir?

Sir Charles

Permit me to suggest the gay Lothario! Or stay! Romeo to Mrs. Woffington's Juliet!

LOVELY PEGGY

Peg

[*To Sir Charles.*]

You are vastly amusing, sir.

[*To Garrick.*]

The Rival Queens is a somewhat heavy tragedy, Mr. Garrick—but if it must be tragedy?

Garrick

Aye, by all means.

Peg

You are the best judge. But a comedy scene?

Garrick

Impossible. I must show them the noblest talent first.

Peg

Shall we recite a scene together—it will encourage you perhaps?

Garrick

Madam, you put me infinitely into your debt.

[*Bows.*]

Rich

Come, Muster Garrick, I can't be waiting here all night.

Peg

Help me to set the stage, Mr. Garrick!

[*Begins to rearrange the furniture with Garrick's help. Sir Charles looks on much amused. Quin snorts and paces up and down. Rich gazes into space and Macklin beams encouragement.*]

Peg

Let me see? Shall we try a scene from the fifth act?

Garrick

I leave it to your judgment, Mrs. Woffington.

Peg

I'll play Roxana to your Alexander. H'm—H'm—no, that scene won't do. That chair should be over on this side, Mr. Garrick. Let us begin with the scene just after I have murdered Statira—you know the place?

Garrick

Certainly. You fling yourself at my feet, dripping blood, and plead for my love.

Sir Charles

That will scarcely give Mrs. Woffington an opportunity to act.

Peg

[*Ignoring the interruption.*]

You spurn me and deliver the long speech about Alexander conquering the world.

LOVELY PEGGY

Sir Charles

Would you play Roxana in breeches, Peg?

Peg

That is easily remedied. I'll throw this cloak about me—
 [*Picks up a cloak and drapes it over her.*]
and let down my hair.
 [*She tosses her wig to one side, takes out some hairpins, shakes her head vigorously and her hair pours over her shoulders.*]

Peg

Now—are you ready, Mr. Garrick?

Garrick

At your service, Mrs. Woffington.

Peg

Will you act as prompter, Mr. Macklin? Have you a text?

Macklin

Text! I know the scene by heart.

Peg

[*Mischievously.*]
Then take care you do not interrupt my grand pause!

LOVELY PEGGY

Quin

Must we witness the mumming of this stroller?

Macklin

Silence, please! Pray begin, Mrs. Woffington.

Peg

[*Assumes the manner of Roxana and begins to declaim in the tragic sing-song of the day.*]

Oh, take me to your arms!
In spite of all your cruelty I love you;
Thus on my knees for ever cling around thee,

[*Kneels at Garrick's feet.*]

'Till you forgive me, or 'till death divide us.

Garrick

[*Assumes a more natural manner as Alexander.*]

Hence, fury, hence: there's not a glance of thine
But like a basilisk comes wing'd with death.

Peg

[*Same business.*]

Oh, speak not thus to one who kneels for mercy!

Garrick

[*Same business.*]

LOVELY PEGGY

Off, murderess, off! for ever shun my sight;
My eyes detest thee, for thy soul is ruin.
Repeated injuries have steel'd my heart,
And I could curse myself for being kind.
If there is any majesty above
That has revenge in store for perjured love,
Send, Heaven, the swiftest ruin on her head!
Is there not cause to put the world in mourning?
Burn all the spires that seem to meet the sky,
And raze the battlements of all the world!

> [*Sir Charles bursts into loud laughter at the conclusion. Then with elaborate politeness he raises Peg to her feet.*]

Sir Charles

'Twas as good as a booth at Bartholomew Fair!
'Twould do for a puppet show, eh, Rich?

Rich

You must larn how to act, Muster Garrick.

Quin

Egad, if you call *that* acting, Mr. Garrick, then we're all wrong.

Macklin

Aye, you may sneer if you will—but my only fear is that this young man will be spoiled, for he will have no competitor.

LOVELY PEGGY

Garrick

Must I speak an epilogue, Mr. Rich—and ask you to grant my suit?

Rich

It's soon spoke. No!

Garrick

What? But I—I—I—

Rich

No!! Do ye hear? No!!
[*Rich stamps out of the room, muttering to himself.*]

Garrick

[*Crestfallen—turning toward Quin.*]
Perhaps you, sir, will be more lenient in your judgment?

Quin

It has seldom been my misfortune, sir, to listen to a person with less talent for the dramatic art!

Garrick

[*Mimicking Quin's voice and manner.*]
Twelve of the clock and a fine night! All's well! Dogberry hath said it!
[*Quin suppresses a muttered oath and stalks from the room.*]

LOVELY PEGGY

Sir Charles

[*Coming up to Garrick.*]

In order to anticipate any more of your impertinent questions, permit me to assure you that your presumption in forcing your way in here is only what is to be expected from a person of your condition.

[*Bows to the others, and goes out, affecting to take snuff. Garrick, pale with rage, is restrained by Peg, who places her hand softly on his arm.*]

Peg

Mr. Garrick, it would ill become you to quarrel with such a man, whose opinion rests upon malice—and jealousy.

Garrick

[*Bowing humbly over her hand.*]

Mrs. Woffington—I—I do not know how to find words which would convey suitably my thanks—

Peg

Then do not try.

Macklin

[*Offers his hand.*]

Mr. Garrick, I have had no small experience on the stage, and my talents—such as they are, sir, have not gone unrewarded. I know an

LOVELY PEGGY

actor when I see one, sir. I was a witness of your performances at Ipswich and I am ready to wager my reputation, sir, on your success.

Garrick

You are very obliging, sir.

Macklin

And furthermore, I will lend you any assistance in my power to secure a London engagement for you.

Peg

And I will do the same! Mr. Giffard of Goodman's Field's Theatre is my friend—I will see him myself!

Garrick

Madam—you—you overwhelm me.

Peg

[*Assuming a broad Irish brogue.*]

Sure, I'm only after helping a fellow artist and it's a thousand pities ye're not Irish like myself—or Mr. Macklin here.

Garrick

What can I say, Mrs. Woffington? After meeting with such rebuffs tonight, to be treated in this manner by you! I see the dreams of my life at last coming true!

LOVELY PEGGY

Macklin

[*Coughs.*]

Then it's settled, my boy. Peggy here and I will try our hand with Giffard, and sure, there ought to be blarney enough between us to get you an engagement.

Garrick

Thank you, Mr. Macklin—really, I—I—

Macklin

Have you thought of a part for your first attempt?

Garrick

Richard the Third I thought most suited to me. I would not like to begin with a part that did not fit my size. If the public expected one of your great hulking heroes—and then I were to step out—I would be laughed off the boards.

Macklin

You're right, Mr. Garrick. Richard the Third is the very thing for you. Perhaps I can find Giffard at the Bedford Coffee House tonight --I'll have a try! Madam, your servant.

[*Bows to Peg.*]

Mr. Garrick!

[*They bow.*]

LOVELY PEGGY

[*Macklin goes out the door R. Peg sits archly on a corner of the table and swings one foot. She draws a piece of paper from the bosom of her coat and reads.*]

Peg

[*Reads.*]

"If truth can fix thy wav'ring heart,
Let Damon urge his claim;
He feels the passion void of art,
A pure and constant flame."

[*Garrick starts when he first hears her, then recites, as she finishes:*]

Garrick

[*Reciting.*]

"Though sighing swains their torments tell,
Their worthless love contemn,
They only prize the beauteous shell
But slight the inward gem."

Peg

It was you who wrote these verses to me then?

Garrick

Did you not observe the initials D. G. at the end?

Peg

And pray are you the only D. G. in London?

LOVELY PEGGY

Garrick

Mrs. Woffington,—if you knew how I have longed for this moment—to meet you face to face,—to hear your voice, to touch your hand! [*Seizes her hand and kisses it.*]

Peg

[*Withdrawing her hand after a moment.*]

You act too well, Mr. Garrick. How shall I believe you?

Garrick

Have I not proved my devotion? Those verses—which you have deigned to treasure—my nightly visits to the theatre to watch your acting,—to follow your every motion on the stage,—I've had eyes for none but you,—you must and shall believe me!

Peg

I thought it was devotion to the art of acting that brought you to the theatre?

Garrick

The art of which you are goddess, and I but the humble worshiper at your shrine!

Peg

[*Sighs.*]

Poor me! The goddess is another being in the green room. Gods and goddesses—kings and

LOVELY PEGGY

queens—we all meet and mingle here—and quarrel for our pitiful share of vanity. Applause is our kingdom—and its echoes soon die.

Garrick

Dear Mrs. Woffington—if you would but hear me!

Peg

[*Smiles.*]

You forget. I am Sir Harry Wildair!

Garrick

To me, a rose by another name. Pity me, most lovely Peggy, for "pity's akin to love."

Peg

[*Suddenly bursts into tears.*]

Have pity on *me!*

[*Recovering herself.*]

There! You may tell the town that you've seen Sir Harry Wildair shed tears.

Garrick

[*Taking her hand again.*]

Forgive me if I wound you with my importunities. Why did you weep?

Peg

Because I am a woman.

Garrick

No better reason?

Peg

There is none.

[*A slight pause.*]

Tell me, what is your opinion of my acting?

Garrick

I beg of you to listen seriously to me!

Peg

Then answer my question. Are you so unskilled as not to know the value of flattery?

Garrick

I cannot flatter you—I—

Peg

What do you say of my Sir Harry Wildair?

Garrick

I—I admire everything you do.

Peg

The truth—what is it?

Garrick

Your acting of Sir Harry is full of spirit, but—

Peg

I know that "but"!—Go on! I command you!

LOVELY PEGGY

Garrick

But after all one knows you to be a woman. You do not play it as a man would.

Peg

The town does not agree with you.

Garrick

The town is the oracle of Delphi—and I speak the words of Cassandra.

Peg

[*Half vexed and half amused.*]
No man ever dared before to tell me to my face that I could not act! Only women have done that!

Garrick

You commanded me to speak the truth!

Peg

And I hold to it. Pray continue. My Sir Harry Wildair is feminine. What next, Sir Critic?

Garrick

Ah, but I would not have you play it like a man! I would not wish my Peggy capable of that!

Peg

Your Peggy! Has your effrontery no bounds?

LOVELY PEGGY

Garrick

It is the way I always think of you. The words slipped out before I was aware. Forgive me.

Peg

[*Softened.*]

It is granted if you will finish your criticism.

Garrick

Whenever I see a woman play a man's part, I think of what Dr. Johnson once said.

Peg

And what was that, pray?

Garrick

That it was very wonderful to see a dog walk upon his hind legs, although he did it very ill. But the marvel was he could do it at all.

Peg

[*Getting off from the table.*]

I vow, Mr. Garrick, if frankness be a virtue—you will get your reward in Heaven!

Garrick

Do not censure me for obeying your command.

Peg

You are vastly impertinent, sir! I am not accustomed to the patronage of—of—

LOVELY PEGGY

Garrick

[*Quietly.*]

Wine-merchants?

Peg

Why, since you will have it so—yes.

Garrick

[*Goes slowly toward door.*]

I am sorry that I gave offence where none was meant. But my sin was to believe that a woman meant what she said. Madam, I have the honor—

Peg

[*Imperiously.*]

Stop!

[*Then with arch demureness.*]

You have not said what you thought of me as Sylvia in The Recruiting Officer!

Garrick

[*Returns with enthusiasm.*]

Thought! I tried to utter my thoughts in those verses! Ah, my lovely Peggy, I thought more than you could guess,—or have the patience to hear! The Comic Muse herself could not have better graced the part! As for your beauty—that, madam, touched my heart like some rare sunset seen at sea. But I fear I weary you—

LOVELY PEGGY

Peg

Tell me more! Ah, Mr. Garrick, what vain folk you must think us! But you cannot understand until you really become one of us, what praise means. There is a charm—a mystery in the art of acting which is indescribable. Out there in the pit sit unknown beings,—we make them laugh or cry at will—think of the power that means! Power over men's souls has something of divinity in it, and it is that power which the actor wields.

Garrick

And then?

Peg

[*With sadness.*]
And then—this!

[*A gesture which includes the green room.*]
The doors are closed—the incense no longer floats upon the air—the offerings and the trappings seem cheap and tawdry—the glamor has gone—and "the rest is silence."

Garrick

[*Deeply moved, takes her hand and kisses it.*]
Madam, you have proved what needed no proof to me—that you have a heart. The town in its ignorance says you are heartless.

LOVELY PEGGY

Peg

[*A sudden revulsion seizing her.*]

The town! Ugh, how I hate it! I am its toy—its plaything—to stroke one moment and cast aside the next. I hate it, *I hate it!*

Garrick

Then why not leave it all, dear Peggy,—come with me—and if love may serve you—

Peg

[*Shakes her head smiling.*]

Leave the stage? No, Mr. Garrick—I have drunk too deep. I could not be happy without the music of applause ringing in my ears.

Garrick

[*Kneeling.*]

Madam, I offer you love—devotion—all that a woman needs—

Peg

Some women—perhaps. But I must have more! I must have life—free—free! You cannot cage me!

Garrick

Then you refuse to marry me?

Peg

[*Looks at him with an odd expression.*]

LOVELY PEGGY

Marry you? You offer *me* marriage? Are you in earnest?

Garrick

Never more so, dear Margaret.

Peg

[*Shudders.*]

To marry me—the Irish beggar girl that sold oranges in the streets of Dublin!—Do you know, Mr. Garrick, many men have talked of love to Peg Woffington—but you are the first who ever made honorable love to me!

[*Covers her face with her hands.*]

Don't! Don't!

Garrick

[*Putting one arm around her gently.*]

It is not too late. The future lies before us—so what does the past, that's gone, matter? I love you, dear.

Peg

[*Looking up at him, her eyes shining.*]

Do you?

Garrick

[*Solemnly.*]

Yes.

Peg

[*With decision.*]

Then I'll never marry you, Mr. Garrick.

LOVELY PEGGY

[*Garrick sorrowfully releases her and goes, with uncertainty, toward the door. Peg watches him closely.*]

Peg

[*As he reaches the door.*]
David!

[*He turns and seeing the expression on her face, rushes to her. They embrace.*]

Peg

I can't let you go, David! Ah, sure, I think it's your blarney caught poor Peg Woffington!

[*He kisses her on the mouth.*]

QUICK CURTAIN

ACT II

SCENE: *The house in Southampton Street, November, 1742. A large room of the period. The furniture is of the time of Queen Anne and must not be confused with the furniture and decoration of the latter half of this century. The severely simple interiors of Adams had not yet come into fashion, and there is a rococo touch in the ornaments. L. placed diagonally across the corner of the room, a lady's dressing table with mirror. The center of the stage is occupied by a large mahogany table. R. an open fireplace with easy chair. R. doors to inner rooms, L. door to passage and street. At rear, two windows, through which one gets a vista of tiled roofs and chimney pots. Over the fireplace hangs Hogarth's portrait of Peg Woffington, and on the mantlepiece are two Chelsea-Derby porcelain sphinxes with Peg Woffington's head replacing the usual sphinx's head. For a general idea of the style of this room, see Aubrey Beardsley's illustrations of Wycherley's "Country Wife." The period illustrated is, of course, before this time, but it is assumed that this house has been built some time, and that the interior has remained unchanged, as is the case with many English houses today. It is just before early candle-light. When the*

LOVELY PEGGY

curtain rises, Peg is seated before the dressing table putting the finishing touches of rouge and powder on her face. Garrick, with a great pile of papers before him, is seated in front of the fire, in the easy chair.

Garrick

Peggy, the critics have surrendered! Listen to what they say of me! Eh, are you attending?

Peg

Do you like my eyebrows in this fashion?

Garrick

Zounds, madam, when I talk to you of my triumphs—you retort with an eyebrow!

Peg

I was forgetting. You have ceased to sigh like a furnace and are now seeking the bubble reputation. My eyebrows are of no consequence.

Garrick

[*Rises and crosses to her.*]

Ah, my love! You are cruel. You are and always will be my lovely Peggy.

Peg

[*She looks up at him relenting.*]

David!

LOVELY PEGGY

[*Caressing him.*]
You shall tell me everything they say of you.

[*They cross with their arms around one another's waists and Garrick sits in the easy chair by the fire, while Peg sits on a little stool at his feet, her chin in her hands, looking into the firelight.*]

Garrick

This is what the *Daily Post* has to say of me, Peggy.

[*Reads.*]

"His reception was the most extraordinary and great that was ever known on such an occasion." Aye, it was, too, Peggy—a dozen dukes at the least computation heard me last night.

Peg

A *graceful* tribute, David.

Garrick

Now for the *Champion*.

[*Takes up another newspaper.*]

"Mr. Garrick's voice is neither whining, bellowing, nor grumbling, but natural in its cadence." I must show that to Quin, Peggy. Mark, it says "natural";—none of your bellowing, Quin, my boy!

LOVELY PEGGY

Peg

You will not convince Quin as easily as you have the town.

Garrick

[*Taking up a paper.*]
Here's another! "There was not one in the house that was not in raptures, and I heard several men of judgment declare it their opinion that nobody ever excelled him." Note—it was men of judgment who said this, Peggy.

Peg

We call them that when they praise us.

Garrick

Tush, they are all skilled critics, Peg. See this!
[*Points to a passage in the paper.*]

Peg

[*Reads.*]
"We are surprised, with so peculiar a genius, how it was possible for him to keep off the stage so long." Ah, David, it makes me almost wish you were not a genius.

Garrick

[*Shocked.*]
And why, my love?

LOVELY PEGGY

Peg

You will think me very foolish, David,—but it all makes me a little jealous.

Garrick

What absurdity! Am I jealous of *your* fame, Peggy? Have I complained because you are the greatest actress in England?

Peg

No—I almost wish you had! Ah, I know it is nonsense I am talking! But, David, when I think of two famous people living together in the same house, it frightens me. There's scarce room left for love.

Garrick

But think how unjust you are! You would only have one of us famous—and that would have to be yourself,—since you were famous before we met. This is selfish of you, Peggy.

Peg

I suppose it is, David, and yet—

Garrick

And yet! Would you give up your fame,—would you leave the stage for my love when I entreated you to do it?

LOVELY PEGGY

Peg

[*Softly.*]

No,—the theatre is in my very blood! I was almost born to it. I remember as a child in Dublin, when I was almost a beggar—I sold oranges and salad in the streets then, David— one day I passed a little booth and I paid away the penny I should have taken home, to see the show inside. A Frenchwoman—Madame Violante she called herself—was performing on the tight rope! I gaped in open-mouthed wonder until she spied me. I was even prettier then than I am now, David, although I was barefooted and in rags.

Garrick

You could not have been more beautiful, Peggy —I won't allow that!

Peg

She asked me if I would like to join her troupe. It seemed as if Heaven was opening before my eyes,—to escape from the life of misery and want—to wear spangles and pretty clothes instead of rags—to dance in a glitter of light instead of crawling home to a dark hovel! From that hour the theatre became my very life,—I have given it even my soul, and you ask me to leave the stage!

LOVELY PEGGY

Garrick

No, no, Peggy, I see it is impossible,—but why, then, complain of my fame?

Peg

Because the theatre did not seek you out; because even with all your fame you are not yet a part of it. You had another life,—you could have been happy without it—

Garrick

No, Peggy, it was stronger than I.

Peg

That is why I am jealous of it! It is going to stand between us, David! As your fame grows greater and greater, my love will mean less and less to you.

Garrick

Never, Peggy, on my faith and honor! You shall always be the first object of my life.

Peg

[*Shakes her head and smiles.*]
David—you do not understand,—you do not realize its power.

Garrick

I will prove to you that I am right.

LOVELY PEGGY

Peg

Then will you marry me, David, at once?

Garrick

If you insist!

Peg

[*Rising.*]
If I insist!

Garrick

Nay, I mean if it will make you happier, Peg. Listen to me, my love. At first I could not marry you—until my means were equal to yours—you agreed to that?

Peg

Yes.

Garrick

And now I have hesitated to disturb our idyl. We are so happy—could any ceremony do more for us than our love has already done?

Peg

I want to feel that you are mine!

Garrick

There is nothing in this world that can make our love more true.

Peg

In that case, you will not deny me what you consider so small a favor?

Garrick

'Faith, Peggy, I have all along intended this very thing; nay, let me convince you.

[*Goes to a desk up stage R., opens a drawer and takes out a little box.*]

Garrick

[*Coming down stage again.*]

Guess what I have here, Peggy!

Peg

[*Fingering a miniature which hangs by a chain about her neck.*]

Some trinket, another miniature perhaps,—to soothe me like a petulant child!

Garrick

You wrong me, Peg. It is not a miniature this time—though, 'faith the one you have is a token of our first love. It's the very ring itself!

Peg

David!

Garrick

Aye—now you are well punished for your doubts!

LOVELY PEGGY

Peg

Oh, forgive me, David, forgive me! I am so happy!

Garrick

Will you try the ring on to see if it fits?

Peg

It's bad luck to do that! Measure my finger with a bit of string.

Garrick

Nonsense,—do you still believe in these Irish fables?

Peg

[*Crosses herself.*]

Hush!

Garrick

Come, let me put it on your finger, Peggy!

Peg

Will you promise to keep away the bad luck, David?

Garrick

[*Draws her to him.*]

No harm shall ever come to my Peggy.

[*Slips the ring on to her finger. She shivers and bursts into tears.*]

LOVELY PEGGY

Peg

I am frightened, David!

Garrick

Be reasonable! What harm can there be in it? To punish you for such superstitions,—you must wear it all the evening. It will proclaim my resolve to our guests tonight.

Peg

Our guests! You've made me so happy I had forgotten them. Where's Pompey? I must dress me quickly—or I shall be too late!

[*Runs to a bell cord and pulls it. Enter a little black boy in Oriental dress.*]

Peg

Quick, Pompey! Tell Hodgson to prepare the table at once! And, Pompey—fetch the candles.

Pompey

Yes, madam.

[*Bows and goes out.*]

Garrick

I hope you have not been extravagant in your preparations?

Peg

What does it matter this once! Think of the

LOVELY PEGGY

occasion—to celebrate your fame—and *this,* for me!

[*Holds up her finger with the ring on it.*]

Garrick

Still we must not let the money run away at too fast a pace.

Peg

It is my turn to pay the bills this month, David, and I promise you shall never even see them. Do not be uneasy on that score.

[*Hastily tidies up the room.*]

Peg

[*Stopping suddenly.*]

David—I had almost forgotten something important! Happiness drove it out of my head.

[*Goes to dresisng table.*]

See—I have a present for you—a gift to bring you luck, because I bought it to mark your success at Drury Lane.

[*Opens box.*]

Diamond shoe buckles!

Garrick

Diamonds! Peggy, you'll be ruined!

Peg

I bought them with my own salary—twenty Sir

LOVELY PEGGY

Harry Wildairs went to the making of them,
—but what did I care, if they were for you!

Garrick

[*Takes them and kisses her.*]
My child! You are recklessly extravagant!

Peg

Don't scold me!

Garrick

Scold you? I can forgive you anything, Peggy.

Peg

[*Slowly, her mood changing suddenly.*]
There's another reason why your ring has made me so happy.

Garrick

What do you mean?

Peg

You must protect me now, David, from the importunities of the green room loungers. Sir Charles has never ceased his—his attentions. He follows me—oh, it's intolerable, David! I did not care to speak of it until you gave me this. I had no claim on your protection. But you must help me, David—you must save me from myself!

LOVELY PEGGY

Garrick

[*Gravely.*]

I am glad you told me. When did you see Sir Charles last?

Peg

Oh, not for an age!

Garrick

And when was that?

Peg

This—this morning—at rehearsal.

Garrick

This morning? You said it was an age!

Peg

[*Demurely.*]

It seemed so, David—because I didn't see you all day!

Garrick

Leave it all to me, my love. I will see that you are spared further annoyance.

[*Enter Pompey with silver candelabra containing lighted candles. He places them about the room. Hodgson, the butler, follows him and they begin to prepare the table.*]

Peg

[*Curtseying with mock formality.*]

LOVELY PEGGY

Will Mr. David Garrick excuse me while I go to put on another dress.

[*He bows in return, and she runs, laughing, out the door, R.*]

Garrick

[*To Pompey.*]

Snuff that candle, Pompey. Can't you see it is burning wastefully?

[*Pompey obeys. Garrick scrutinizes the arrangement of the table.*]

Garrick

Sweetmeats, Hodgson, for supper!

Hodgson

Mrs. Woffington's commands, sir.

Garrick

Lord, what extravagance! Remember, Hodgson, when it is my month to pay the bills, you are on no account to serve sweetmeats at supper.

Hodgson

Very well, sir.

[*A loud knocking is heard at the outer door.*]

Garrick

Show the gentleman in here directly, Hodgson.

LOVELY PEGGY

Hodgson

Yes, sir.

[*He goes out and returning, ushers in Charles Macklin.*]

Macklin

Ah, Davy, my boy! And how does it feel to be famous, sir?

Garrick

To tell the truth, Macklin, it feels very little different from being a wine-merchant.

Macklin

[*Sits in front of the fire and warms his hands.*]

Aye, there's no end to either position. By the bye, Davy, where's Mrs. Woffington?

Garrick

She will join us later.

Macklin

Well, I confess that I hardly expected Peg to turn out a pattern of domestic virtue, eh, Garrick!

Garrick

Sir, I do not know what you mean.

Macklin

Only the impertinence of an old friend. How long is this—er—to continue?

LOVELY PEGGY

Garrick

Upon my word, sir, you take strange liberties with our friendship.

Macklin

No offence, Davy, no offence! You have been living together about six months now?

Garrick

Ever since we began the season together in Dublin last summer.

Macklin

Ah. You saw nothing of Sir Charles Hanbury Williams in Ireland, I presume?

Garrick

Damme, Macklin, what are you driving at?

Macklin

My boy, when you have been on the stage as long as I have,—why, you will not have so many illusions left. You believe seriously that this woman loves you?

Garrick

Yes. Whatever she may have been once, she is now the soul of honor.

Macklin

Davy, beware the leopard's spots! 'Tis not the animal intended for domesticity.

LOVELY PEGGY

Garrick

Confound your cynicism, sir! You—you—you've quite spoiled my temper.

Macklin

Tush! Take care, Davy, that you don't spoil your whole life.

Garrick

The lady against whom you are trying to poison my mind, sir, is going to become my wife!

Macklin

[*Jumps up.*]
Good God, Davy! Are you serious?

Garrick

Never more so.

Macklin

In that event, I will say no more.
[*Offers his hand.*]
I trust that you will never have cause to repent your judgment.
[*Garrick takes his hand.*]

Garrick

Are you keeping anything back from me, Macklin?

Macklin

Nothing positive. Only some advice which you do not seem inclined to take.

LOVELY PEGGY

Garrick

You have no assertion which you are prepared to prove?

Macklin

None but gossip—and you know the value of that as well as I. But if Hamlet were here today instead of "frailty, thy name is woman," he would say, "frailty, thy name is Woffington!"

Garrick

Change it to "was" and I grant it.

Macklin

Sir Charles was at the rehearsal this morning—during your absence.

Garrick

She has already told me that—and begged me to protect her from his unwelcome attentions.

Macklin

The clever Irish jade! Davy, I'm a descendant of an Irish king myself, and know my own country-people as no Sassenach ever can. And beware of blarney in whatever form you find it.

Garrick

Mr. Macklin, only our long friendship and your age has made me listen to you with patience, but the latter is fast becoming exhausted.

LOVELY PEGGY

Macklin

My only defence is my interest in your welfare. I shall continue to have that admiration for Mrs. Woffington which I have always shown her. You need not be uneasy—and I'll contradict the malice of the town whenever I hear it.

Garrick

A glass of wine, sir?

Macklin

[*Rising.*]

Sir, if you please!

[*Garrick pours two glasses of wine and they drink to one another with great solemnity. A loud knocking is heard, off, and in a moment Hodgson ushers in Dr. Samuel Johnson.*]

Hodgson

[*Announcing.*]

Dr. Samuel Johnson.

[*The latter enters noisily, puffing and stamping his feet. His hat he hands to Hodgson, but his heavy stick he keeps with him.*]

Garrick

Sir, welcome to my house. This, sir, is Mr. Macklin, of whom you have heard me speak. A fellow actor and comedian.

LOVELY PEGGY

Johnson

Sir, fortune has tempted you to a luxury not becoming your position in society.
[*Surveying the room.*]
When I came up to London with Davy, I had only twopence halfpenny in my pocket.

Garrick

Eh? What do you say? With twopence halfpenny in your pocket?

Johnson

Why, yes; and thou, Davy, with three halfpence in thine.

Garrick

You do not allow, sir, any reward to merit?

Johnson

Why, yes, sir, I do. But a stage player has no merit. He is a parasite. You exist by repeating the thoughts of others and have none of your own. You have a kind of rant, with which you run on, without any regard either to accent or emphasis.

Garrick

Sir, Mr. Macklin and myself I hold to be better judges of this art than you.

LOVELY PEGGY

Johnson

Well, now, I'll give you something to speak, with which you are little acquainted, and then we shall see how just my observation is. Let me hear you repeat the ninth Commandment.

Garrick

"Thou shalt not bear false witness against thy neighbor."

Johnson

Wrong, sir! Wrong! The accent should come equally upon the words "shalt" and "not."

[*Chuckles and stamps with his cane.*]

You are not too old to take a lesson from me still, Davy.

Garrick

You must come to the green room more often that we may benefit by your critical taste.

Johnson

Nay, Davy, I'll come no more to your green room. The white bosoms and silk stockings of your actresses arouse my amorous spirit.

[*He renews his survey of the room. Picks up a handsome china cup on the table.*]

Garrick

Pray, be careful, sir, of that cup, as you are not accustomed to handling fine china.

LOVELY PEGGY

Johnson

[*Dropping it and letting it smash.*]

Sir, I smashed your cup as a lesson to you that such things have no value in themselves but only a fictitious worth which vanity gives them.

[*Stamps over to the mantlepiece and takes the china sphinx with Peg Woffington's head on it off the shelf.*]

Garrick

Sir, I implore you not to break that as well!

Johnson

[*Holding it up and looking at it critically.*]

I have too much respect, sir, for a woman to imperil even her image. A very good likeness of Mrs. Woffington!

Macklin

Aye, these china figures are the fashion at present. And Mrs. Woffington decrees the fashion for all the town.

Johnson

And Davy here appears to follow all of its decrees!

[*Changing the subject—to Garrick.*]

Sir, have you perused my play?

LOVELY PEGGY

Garrick

[*Goes to the desk and returns with a manuscript.*]

Dr. Johnson, I have studied your tragedy "Irene" carefully and regret that, in its present form, it is not possible to produce it.

Johnson

How not possible?

Garrick

I mean without certain alterations.

Johnson

Alterations, sir? I will never consent, sir, to any alterations whatever.

Garrick

I would suggest that if Mahomet were to go mad at last—and if a new title could be found—

Johnson

Sir, I will not listen to you!

[*To Macklin.*]

I cannot bear that my tragedy should be revised and altered at the pleasure of an actor. Sir, the fellow wants me to make Mahomet run mad, that he may have an opportunity of tossing his hands and kicking his heels in playing it.

LOVELY PEGGY

[*A knock at the door, off. Enter Hodgson, followed by James Quin and George Anne Bellamy.*]

Hodgson
[*Announcing.*]

Mrs. Bellamy! Mr. Quin!

[*They enter and exchange greetings. Pompey enters bringing more candles.*]

Garrick

Pompey, inform your mistress that our guests await her pleasure.

[*Pompey goes out door, right.*]

Quin
[*To Garrick.*]

Sir, I felicitate you upon your triumph and trust that the past may be forgotten.

Garrick

With all my heart!

[*They bow. Enter Peg Woffington, radiantly beautiful in a magnificent dress. All turn to greet her.*]

Macklin

Madam, your devoted slave!

[*Kisses her hand. Quin does the same.*]

Bellamy
[*Embracing her.*]

Ma chère! How beautiful you are!

LOVELY PEGGY

Peg

What a superb dress, my dear! Such charming taste!

[*Dr. Johnson alone remains seated. Peg goes to him.*]

Peg

Dr. Johnson, Mr. Garrick and I are indeed honored by your visit.

Johnson

Madam, the honor is of small consequence.

[*Hodgson enters.*]

Hodgson

[*Announcing.*]

Supper is served.

[*Peg seats herself at the head of the table, with Dr. Johnson on her right. Garrick is at the other end, with Mrs. Bellamy next to him. Macklin and Quin are between Bellamy and Dr. Johnson, facing the audience. Hodgson and Pompey together serve the supper. A large silver tea-urn is placed in front of Peg.*]

Quin

Faith, I'm vastly sorry, Macklin, that your last comedy didn't bring you more pleasure and profit.

LOVELY PEGGY

Macklin

I'm much obliged, but the public taste has been spoiled for originality by the plagiarized rubbish forced down its throat.

Garrick

When may we hope to have a comedy from your pen, Quin?

Quin

What is the use of my writing a comedy, when we have no actors today to play it?

Macklin

Why, there's Garrick here and myself—not to mention the ladies—

Quin

I know your *dramatis personæ* well enough, but damme, where are your actors?

Peg

A cup of tea, Mr. Quin?

Quin

Madam, with pleasure.
[*The cup is passed to him.*]

Johnson

Sir, may I ask you if the world revolves around the stage?

LOVELY PEGGY

Garrick

Why, sir, what do you mean?

Johnson

To listen to the conversation since coming to this house one would think so. Whereas a player, sir, is a fellow who claps a hump on his back, and a lump on his leg, and cries "I am Richard the Third."

Peg

Dr. Johnson, may I offer you a cup of tea?
[*He bows and she hands him a cup.*]

Macklin

[*To Johnson.*]
And where, sir, is your friend Mr. Boswell this evening?

Johnson

Sir, I came to this house for relaxation.

Bellamy

Dr. Johnson, it seems wonderful to me that a man could think of enough words to make a dictionary.

Garrick

Madam, it took forty Frenchmen to write a dictionary of that language:

Talk of war with a Briton, he'll boldly advance
That one English soldier will beat ten of France;
Would we alter the boast from the sword to the pen,
Our odds are still greater, still greater our men;
And Johnson, well arm'd like a hero of yore,
Has beat forty French, and will beat forty more!

[*All applaud and Johnson, who is not deaf to flattery, is obviously pleased.*]

Quin

[*To Garrick.*]

Sir, did you make that up extempore?

Peg

Mr. Quin, epigrams are like woman's beauty—they should be judged by their effect. Let the source of both remain a mystery.

Macklin

In that case, madam, you forbid us to ask whether nature or art is the more important?

Peg

For the making of epigrams?

Macklin

No, madam, for a woman's beauty.

Peg

Nature gives us the garden, but art waters it, sir.

Quin

Dr. Johnson, sir, what is your opinion of our dramatic critics?

Johnson

Why, sir, that a critic may spend his time more profitably in his library than at the theatre.

Macklin

Critics? There are a few doers of newspapers, who call themselves critics, that may still be found in upper boxes—but they reserve their criticisms for the newspapers of the next day; where they come out in columns, sir—columns, often disgraceful as to truth, as they are ignorant of the rules of science.

Quin

Aye, in our time the audiences were judicious. We had few riots and disorders such as are now common at our playhouses.

Bellamy

Is nothing better now than it used to be?

LOVELY PEGGY

Quin

Nothing, madam. We live in a degenerate age. The acting of today is heresy.

Garrick

Pope Quin damns all Churches but his own.
When Doctrines meet with general approbation,
It is not heresy, but reformation.

Macklin

Hear, hear! Sir, your health!
[*All rise.*]
I drink to
>   Roscius, Paris of the stage,
>   Born to please a learned age!

All

To Roscius! Garrick! etc.
[*They drink and sit again.*]

Garrick

[*Rising.*]
My friends, I thank you.

All

Hear, hear!

Garrick

[*Sips a cup of tea.*]
Madam, this tea is as red as blood! It is needless waste to make it so strong!

LOVELY PEGGY

Peg

You can retrieve the loss, sir, next month!

Garrick

[*Picks up a wine-glass and addresses the table.*]

I shall take this opportunity to propose another health—that of Mrs. Woffington!—

All

Hear, hear!

Garrick

Mrs. Woffington—my lovely Peggy—who has honored me with the promise of her hand—to the future Mrs. Garrick!

[*General applause.*]

Garrick

With your permission—we'll celebrate the event with a few verses, which I have kept as a surprise for lovely Peggy.

[*Clears his throat and chants.*]

> Once more I'll tune my vocal shell,
> To hills and dales my passion tell,
> A flame which time may never quell,
>   That burns for lovely Peggy.
>
> The sun first rising in the morn,
> That paints the dew-bespangled thorn,
> Doth not so much the day adorn
>   As does my lovely Peggy.

LOVELY PEGGY

All

Bravo! Bravo!

[*They rise and pick up their glasses.*]

To lovely Peggy!

Garrick

[*As they drink.*]

> While bees from flowers to flowers rove,
> And linnets warble through the grove,
> Or stately swans the waters love,
> So long shall I love Peggy.

[*At the conclusion of the song, Garrick drains his glass and snaps the stem. The others do likewise, and Peggy, very happy and charming in her confusion, rises to reply.*]

Peg

My friends—we poor players are so accustomed to have words put into our mouths for us,—that we lack words of our own. What can I say more than that I am happy? Happy in our love—and happy in the triumph which has been David's on the stage. Alexander sighed for more worlds to conquer. I am happy in having conquered a woman's world—which is love. I sigh for no more. In future this house will be my world, an empire wide enough for me, and when the curtain falls—as some day it must—for the last time—I will be content if I played my part well. Once more, dear friends, I—I thank you.

[*Sits amid general cheers. Both she and Garrick are much moved.*]

Johnson

Madam, permit me to offer my felicitations. I have known Davy Garrick longer than you have. He has wit and genius—and I know him to have a heart.

[*Rises from his chair.*]

And now, madam, I must bid you adieu. I am not accustomed to the late hours which compose the actor's day. Madam, your humble and obedient.

[*Peg rises as do the rest of the company. Dr. Johnson stamps toward the door L. followed by Garrick, amid the farewells of the others. At the door he again pauses and bows with dignity, and then goes out.*]

Bellamy

[*Crosses to Peg.*]

Mrs. Woffington—I wish you every happiness and joy.

Peg

You are very kind, my child. Let us forget all the little differences of the past. Will you forgive me my former rudeness?

Bellamy

With all my heart!

[They kiss and Quin and Macklin also come up and kiss Peg's hand.]

Bellamy

Good night, Mrs. Woffington.

Peg

Good night!

Quin

Madam, I am a crusty old bachelor with a sharp tongue,—but you may count me your friend.

Peg

I will, Mr. Quin, I will.

[Quin escorts Mrs. Bellamy to the door. Garrick sees them out. Macklin stands by Peg talking to her as they go.]

Macklin

Madam, remember that happiness is hard to win and easy to lose. It also entails mutual obligations. One cannot be happy alone. You are in love with genius.

Peg

You speak like Sir Oracle!

Macklin

I am. I have lived, Mrs. Woffington. They call me a man of the last century.

LOVELY PEGGY

Peg

[*Roguishly.*]

I have heard they called you the Wild Irishman!

Macklin

That too.

Peg

But what is this riddle you have propounded to me?

Macklin

Madam, you must guess the answer for yourself.
[*Bows.*]
Good night.

[*As he goes, Hodgson and Pompey rapidly clear the table. Peg sits in the chair before the fire and Garrick returns to her.*]

Peg

What an odd character Macklin is!

Garrick

[*Starts.*]
Why do you say that, Peggy?

Peg

He has been speaking to me in riddles. I could not understand what he meant. He warned me to take care—of what, David—do you know?

LOVELY PEGGY

Garrick

Give it no thought, Peggy. He likes to affect the cynic.

Peg

He frightened me—I don't know why. You love me, David?

Garrick

Can you ask?

Peg

I am foolish—forgive me—but it is such joy to hear you say it.

[The servants go out, having completed the clearing of the table, which they shove back up stage, leaving more of the center clear.]

Garrick

My angel!

[Kisses her hand.]

I—I must leave you awhile now, Peggy. I have an appointment at the Bedford,—it is on business connected with the theatre.

Peg

I shall come to hate the theatre, David! It is always coming between us and stealing away our most precious moments.

Garrick

[Consults his watch.]

LOVELY PEGGY

I will not be long, dearest. It is very late.

[*Kisses her on the forehead and goes, leaving her sitting before the fire.*]

[*Enter after a brief pause, Pompey. He comes forward mysteriously.*]

Pompey

Missis!

[*Peg starts. She had not been aware of his entrance.*]

Peg

How you startled me, Pompey! What is it?

Pompey

Sh! Master gone away?

Peg

Your master has gone to the Bedford.

Pompey

Then me give you this.

[*Produces a note with an air of triumph. Peg takes it.*]

Peg

Who gave you this, Pompey?

Pompey

Fine gentleman! Gave Pompey a guinea—all gold,—he said take note Mrs. Woffington—

LOVELY PEGGY

your mistress—give it her when she alone—or he break every bone in Pompey's body!

Peg

You may go, Pompey.

Pompey

Thank you, missis.

[*Goes out door, L.*]

Peg

[*When he has gone, breaks the seal and goes to a candle to read it.*]

To the beautiful but cruel Mrs. Woffington. The man you believe perfect and who tells you of his love, has a different tale to tell behind your back. Ask the beautiful V. who dances at Drury Lane, if she knows one David Garrick. (Signed) C.

It's monstrous! It's a lie! It's another trick of Sir Charles. Does he think he can trap me so easily?

[*She starts to burn the letter at the fire; then hesitates and puts it in her bosom. She sits again in the large armchair with her back to the door L. The latter is quietly opened and Sir Charles glides noiselessly into the room, after closing the door carefully behind him. He tiptoes to the chair, stoops suddenly and kisses Peg. She springs to her feet with a scream.*]

LOVELY PEGGY

Peg

You!

Sir Charles

Yes, my soul's idol, it is I.

Peg

How dare you force your way in here! My servants shall throw you into the street.
[*Rushes toward bell rope.*]

Sir Charles

It would be folly to inform them of my presence. They would undoubtedly communicate the fact to Mr. Garrick.

Peg

[*Pausing.*]
How did you get in?

Sir Charles

I have been watching from the street. Mr. Garrick is careless—very careless. He left the front door ajar.

Peg

You must leave this house instantly.

Sir Charles

Pardon me, I will leave it when I choose.
[*Pours himself a glass of wine.*]

LOVELY PEGGY

To our future meetings!
 [*Drinks.*]

Peg

[*Takes hold of bell rope.*]
I will ring for help then! I'll tell how you forced your way in here—

Sir Charles

I would not risk it, Peg. Really, I wouldn't. Mr. Garrick is a jealous man—and I might remind you that he has had cause to be jealous of me before.

Peg

[*Pauses by the bell.*]
You are a monster—a beast!

Sir Charles

[*Continues to drink.*]
A basilisk—or what you will. By the bye, Peggy, it was very careless of you in the old days to send me love letters undated.

[*Takes out one or two letters.*]
I have some with me to which I have been careful to have the date added—a recent date, you understand? Now ring the bell, for I am anxious to show these letters to friend Davy myself. Let us send Pompey to the Bedford to fetch him.

LOVELY PEGGY

Peg

You are heartless!

Sir Charles

[*All through this scene he is gradually becoming intoxicated.*]

As heartless now as you have been to me. Madam, you were pleased to throw me over for a wine-merchant. You are now to reap the consequences of your folly.

Peg

Have you no pity? Will nothing move you?

Sir Charles

Nothing. I have not come to make terms but to demand them. If you become my mistress again—

Peg

I never was your mistress—

Sir Charles

I prefer to call it that—the world would see little distinction in these titles. What it believed you to be before, by Heaven, I'm going to make you now!

Peg

And if I refuse?

Sir Charles

In that case I will put these letters into Garrick's hands.

Peg

Do it! I defy you. If you are so base as to ruin my life because I was once fool enough to trust you, do it! But you won't conquer me though you overturn my castle!

Sir Charles

You lack the courage to resist me. I will break you down, Peg. You love praise and flattery —you cannot live without them. It's your very life. I'll give you both. Garrick is growing tired of you.

[*Peg winces.*]

Ah, that went home did it? You received my note, I see.

Peg

I received your lies which you bribed my servant to give me. But they are lies. See this ring! It was placed on my finger today and if you dare to tell your lies to my husband, he'll kill you!

Sir Charles

Your husband!

[*Laughs.*]

Where may I go to hear the banns read? Eh,

LOVELY PEGGY

Peggy? The gift appears to me suited to the well-known parsimony of our friend! Send it to the jewelers and make certain it isn't brass!

Peg

Our betrothal was announced to our friends in this very room tonight.

Sir Charles

Aye, that's it, Peggy, my dear. David has many friends but no friend. If you don't believe me, watch him for yourself. Have you seen the fair Mademoiselle Violette? Ah, I see you know her.

Peg

What of that?

Sir Charles

Simply this. Your—er—what is it you call him—ah, yes, husband—wasn't that what you said? Husband has a pleasant sound!—Well, your husband—no, hang it, I won't call him that! Mr. Punch, the play-actor, knows Mademoiselle Violette.

Peg

It is not surprising. She dances at Drury Lane.

Sir Charles

She'll lead him a dance, never you fear, and you, too, Peggy.

LOVELY PEGGY

Peg

Because you are incapable of honor yourself, you impute dishonor to everyone else.

Sir Charles

No, Peg, you're wrong there. You can see for yourself that vanity is devouring him. Pretty women by the dozen are at his feet. It takes a greater man that Davy Garrick to say, "get you behind me, ladies." I know you both, Peg. You won't tolerate Davy—because you've let him make a fool of you. And he will weary of you because you were the first— and no famous man ever lives with his first love!

[*Laughs at his own joke.*]

Confess, Peggy, you are beginning to believe me in the right?

Peg

No! It is all lies from beginning to end!

Sir Charles

There! You see you know what to expect from me. But with a man like Punch you never know where to look for him next. I saw your Garrick and this Mademoiselle Violette in the green room the other day, whispering behind her fan.

LOVELY PEGGY

Peg

If you hope to make me jealous, you are wasting your breath.

Sir Charles

Very well, we'll grant him Mademoiselle Violette. Nay, Peggy, you shall listen to me! I love you—I tell you I do! Damme, I've known too many women not to pick a thoroughbred when I see one. You've wit and pluck, too, by Jove, beauty—everything I want. The conjunction is a rare one. I can pick you a dozen pretty faces and a dozen witty minds, but they don't often go together. There's Bellamy—a doll—pretty, if you like—none prettier—but, Peggy, the girl is intolerably dull—silly—vain—affected. I made her a present of two hundred pounds and bowed myself out.

[*Sits in a chair and stretches himself comfortably.*]

What a soundless depth between the Bellamy and you! You know, I have leisure to appreciate a woman.—I've no occupation to use up my life and its most precious moments. I've my estate, a baronetcy is a comfortable, inconspicuous title. One is not expected to be famous if one is merely a baronet.

Peg

You seem to prefer to be infamous.

LOVELY PEGGY

Sir Charles

You do me wrong, Peg, 'pon my honor, you do. I confess I seek pleasure where I can find it—but through it all runs my love for you—like the burden of a song. Egad, you make me serious. It's a compliment, Peg. No other woman can do it.

Peg

Sir, your insolence and conceit—

Sir Charles

Ah, I know all about them, too. But I'm not in love with fame—I'm not in love with vanity—and that play-acting fellow is! I'm in love with you—but he's in love with himself.

Peg

Won't you go, sir? Haven't you tortured me enough?

Sir Charles

Go? Not I. You compel me to stay. I wish to show Mr. Garrick some private correspondence.

[*Takes another glass of wine.*]

Peg

I—I am fighting hard to do my duty,—and you come here as if to punish me for my sins! Will you take this last opportunity from me to

LOVELY PEGGY

redeem myself? I love David Garrick. What am I to you? There are a dozen women who can give you more than I can,—you have wealth, power, everything. As for me, I was a beggar girl once,—why should you even stoop to notice me? You have your own world to live in. Leave me to live in mine. Mr. Garrick says he loves me and will marry me. Would you do the same?

Sir Charles

[*Drinking.*]

Marry you, Peg? I would be the laughing-stock of the town!

Peg

[*Winces.*]

Is that the penalty you pay for seeking my society?

Sir Charles

[*Takes a drink.*]

It's fashionable to run after actresses,—I like cards better myself—but must be fashionable. You most fashionable actress in town. Hence must run after you. That's excellent wine, Peg. Not fashionable to marry actresses.

Peg

At last I am to hear the truth, am I?

LOVELY PEGGY

Sir Charles

Egad, always tell the truth, Peg—and nobody will believe you. Excellent rule. I tell you what I'll do. I'll settle an annuity on you, Peg—five hundred pounds a year and damme, that's generous.

[*Peg endeavors to pick up the letters which he had laid beside the arm of his chair, but with a drunkard's cunning he is too quick for her and puts them in his side pocket.*]

Sir Charles

Sly, eh, Peggy? Sly? Too old a dog, Peg. I'm too old a dog. No, we'll read 'em to Master Davy when he comes home. Egad, I hope I shan't laugh when I see his face.

[*Peg is getting very nervous and almost desperate. She goes to window and peers up the street. Then returns and stands irresolute a second, watching Sir Charles drinking still another glass of wine. She goes up stage and returns with another decanter which she sets before him.*]

Peg

An annuity, I think you said?

[*Pours him out a glass from the new decanter.*]

LOVELY PEGGY

Sir Charles

Five hundred pounds—that's it.

> [*She comes close to him and he fingers the miniature hanging by a chain around her neck.*]

Devilish pretty miniature, Peg!

Peg

> [*Shudders and tries to make him release the miniature.*]

Will you give me your opinion of this brandy?

Sir Charles

> [*He releases the miniature.*]

Brandy? Let me have it.

> [*She hands him the glass. He sniffs the bouquet and spills a little.*]

You sly puss! It's the money caught you— damme, money always catches 'em. An' I waste time making love!

> [*Tries to catch her around the waist but she eludes him.*]

I'll see my lawyer about it in mornin', 'pon honor. Five hundreds pounds—all yours—give me another glass.

Peg

> [*Pours him a glass.*]

You really thought I was in earnest when I refused you?

[*He nods his head solemnly.*]

Fie, Sir Charles—and you pretend to understand women!

Sir Charles

It's mistake—I don't—nobody does. It's money—

[*Nods and falls asleep. She watches him a moment and as he begins to snore, tiptoes up and carefully removes the letters from his pocket, where he had put them. With a quick movement she darts across the stage and places them in the fire. She makes certain that they blaze up and when the flicker of the flames has died away, she returns to where Sir Charles is sitting. She shakes him, but it has no effect. She goes then to the dressing table up-stage and returns with a bottle of sal volatile. She sprinkles it vigorously full in his face. With a start and a suppressed exclamation he wakes up and staggers to his feet.*]

Sir Charles

What the devil!

[*Sneezes violently several times, while Peg plies the smelling salts.*]

Damme—what's the matter?

LOVELY PEGGY

[*Sneeze.*]

Where am I?

[*Sneeze.*]

Peg

[*Putting the bottle down.*]

The Irish girl was too much for ye that time, me fine gentleman. The letters are burnt—and now I won't be keeping you any longer, Sir Charles!

[*He searches his pockets and the table hastily. The sal volatile has sobered him.*]

Peg

I hope you like the flavor of my smelling salts!

Sir Charles

[*Advances threateningly.*]

Give me back the letters!

[*He seizes her roughly in his arms, while she struggles with him. His wig comes off in the tussle.*]

Peg

[*Fighting him off.*]

The letters are in the fire! Now go! Or I summon the household!

[*The front door is heard to slam. Peg starts and in an agony of fear shoves Sir Charles toward the door R.*]

LOVELY PEGGY

Peg

There's a way out through the passage at the other side. If he finds you here I swear he will kill you!

Sir Charles

[*Draws his sword coolly.*]

'Faith, killing is a game two can play at.

[*He tests his blade and strikes an attitude. Peg rushes across the room and locks the door into the hall.*]

Not so eager for the slaughter as you were?

[*The door is tried and rattled. Garrick's voice is heard.*]

Open, Peggy, open! Are you asleep, my love?

Sir Charles

Shall I trouble you to unlock that door, or shall I do it myself?

[*Takes a step toward it.*]

Peg

Oh—go—go!

[*Garrick's voice.*]

Within there! Peggy! Open—it's David!

Sir Charles

The next time he calls, I'll answer for you.

Peg

[*Clinging to him.*]

If you'll only go—I'll promise anything—anything!

Sir Charles

I've given too many of them myself to value them much.

[*Takes the miniature and chain off her neck—reads inscription on back.*]

"To lovely Peggy from David," that will do. If you come to claim this, it shall be yours. If you don't I'll tell your David that you gave it to me!

[*Garrick's voice off.*]

Open!

[*He knocks loudly.*]

Sir Charles

[*Bows.*]

To our future meeting!

[*He slips through the door R. and Peggy turns the key after him.*]

[*Garrick's voice.*]

Hodgson!—Pompey!

[*Peg goes to door L., and opens it, yawning in Garrick's face as he rushes in followed by Pompey and Hodgson in strange night attire.*]

LOVELY PEGGY

Peg

Oh, 'tis you, David! You're very late.

Garrick

Late! Egad, I've been halloing and knocking these ten minutes. Gabriel himself could not have made more noise.

Peg

I must have been asleep. I heard nothing until this moment when you called out to the servants, didn't you?
[*Yawns.*]

Garrick

[*To Pompey and Hodgson.*]
Well, what do you stand gaping at? You may go, both of you.
[*They go out and Garrick closes the door.*]

Peg

The wine must have made me sleepy. Did you finish your business at the Bedford?

Garrick

[*His eyes taking in the room.*]
Aye. It was soon finished.—Peg, I thought I heard voices in this room while I was outside.

LOVELY PEGGY

Peg

Voices? Perhaps I talked in my sleep, Davy. I was sitting here before the fire and it was dull waiting for you. I was a bit drowsy.

Garrick

[*Stopping by the decanters.*]
You've been drinking brandy, Peg?

Peg

Yes, I felt a little chilly after you went. There's nothing like brandy for the stomach, Davy.

Garrick

[*Takes out his handkerchief and measures the liquid remaining in the decanter.*]
'Faith, Peggy, I don't wonder you were drowsy. It has fallen a good three inches.

Peg

You measure the wine?

Garrick

You would not permit the servants to rob you, I suppose?

Peg

But it is my turn to pay this month!

Garrick

All the more reason for me to see that Hodgson or Pompey do not impose upon your good

LOVELY PEGGY

nature. Three inches of brandy is worth two shillings—no, 'tis a half crown. At that rate a guinea is soon gone to the devil.

Peg

Trust you, Davy, for making it go further than anyone else!

[*Garrick walks about the room nervously, Peg watching him anxiously. As he does so, he stumbles across Sir Charles' wig which lies under one corner of the table.*]

Garrick

[*Stooping and picking up the wig.*]
What's this?
[*Holds it up.*]
A man's wig!
[*Examines it hastily.*]
It's not my wig!

Peg

[*Coolly.*]
No, it is not!

Garrick

[*Getting very much excited.*]
Oh, madam, I have found you out at last? So there has been another lover in the case!
[*Working himself into a passion.*]

LOVELY PEGGY

You've made a fool of me before the town! Your intrigues and extravagances are the common gossip of the Bedford! I hear men sneer behind my back when I come into a room. And now you dare to meet your lovers in our very house! That was why the door was locked on my return!

Peg

[*With dangerous calmness.*]

I beg of you, Mr. Garrick, not to make of yourself so great a fool! Please give me my wig back again.

Garrick

What! Madam, do you glory in your infidelity? Do you own the wig then?

Peg

Yes, to be sure I do. I'm sure it was my money paid for it, and I hope it will repay me with money and reputation, too.

Garrick

[*Taken aback at her coolness.*]

Madam, what do you mean? Explain yourself, if you can.

Peg

When you are in a more sensible frame of mind I will give you an explanation, not before.

LOVELY PEGGY

Garrick

Zounds, madam, do not torture me in this way! I demand—nay, I entreat you will explain the presence of this strange wig in our apartment?

Peg

Why, if you thus choose to desert your character as a man and insist upon prying into all my business, know that it is a new wig which I ordered for my part of Sir Harry Wildair—and since you chose to leave me to myself this evening—I have been rehearsing in it before going to bed. I was careless enough to leave it in your way—but is that a reason to scold and plague me as if I were a common—

Garrick

But the door, madam! How do you explain the fact that it was locked upon my return?

Peg

Because I do not wish to remain alone in the house without some protection.

Garrick

[*Dropping on one knee.*]

It was wrong of me to doubt you. I've been so tormented by my jealousy of you! Everywhere I turn our enemies and detractors spread lies and scandal—

LOVELY PEGGY

Peg

If you listen to them instead of me!

Garrick

Nay, Peggy, I'll never give them another thought! I swear it! I will believe you and only you! Say that you love me!

Peg

I will not say it again until you have given me proof of one thing. Do you love me, David?

Garrick

My dearest, how can you ask? Have I not proved it again and again?

Peg

There is one final proof that you must give me at once. David, you must make an honest woman of me. There must be no more delay, or I won't answer for the consequences!

Garrick

Peg!

Peg

I mean it, David. You must give me your promise tonight, once for all!

Garrick

But I have given it to you! Did I not announce it to all our friends?

Peg

I want to know when it is to be.

Garrick

Then, on my honor, it shall be as soon as we can have the banns read! I'll have them posted tomorrow.

Peg

David!

[*He puts his arm around her waist and they sit before the fire together.*]

And you'll marry the Irish beggar girl?

Garrick

Yes—and, Peggy, we will buy ourselves an estate in the country—say, up the river somewhere,—and live monarchs of all we survey! We'll laugh at the town—aye, and at the critics too! Nothing shall disturb our arcadian bliss.

Peg

I shall keep fowls, David. I've always wanted to.

Garrick

Excellent! And I, let me think—ah, yes, I will build a little temple to Shakespeare in the garden and we will sit in it on summer evenings and play Romeo and Juliet to the moon.

[*A short pause, Garrick looks at Peg's neck.*]

LOVELY PEGGY

Let me have the miniature you wear about your neck, Peg. I'll have a jewel added to it to mark this night.

Peg

[*Changing color.*]
Not that, Davy! It must be something new!

Garrick

Nay, I am determined. At least, let me see it and show you where I mean to place it.

Peg

I took it off, it is locked up with my jewels.

Garrick

But you were wearing it before I left.

Peg

I know, but I locked my jewels away for the night.

Garrick

Strange—here is a diamond pin, and here's a chain of pearls about your neck!

Peg

I am sleepy, David! Would you plague me for a trinket tonight?

Garrick

Nay, give me your key and I will fetch it out for you.

LOVELY PEGGY

Peg

I have forgotten where I put the key. On the mantelpiece perhaps.

Garrick

[*A look of suspicion growing again in his face.*]
On the mantel you said?

Peg

Or in my room.
  [*He goes to the door of her room and tries it. It is locked.*]

Garrick

How's this, madam? Your room locked too?

Peg

Of course. The back stairs lead into the passage beyond, and I was afraid, David, all alone.
  [*Garrick unlocks the door and opens it quickly. As he does so a sheet of paper pinned to the other side of the door, flutters to the floor. Peg sees it and springs to her feet with a little cry, then recovers herself quickly and stands watching Garrick with panting bosom. Deliberately he picks the paper up and reads it.*]

LOVELY PEGGY

Garrick

[*Reading.*]

"To Master Davy Garrick: Should you wish to reclaim a certain miniature belonging to Mrs. Woffington, the undersigned will deliver it to you. I have the honor to remain, your humble,

Hanbury Williams."

[*A look of rage and jealousy comes into Garrick's face. Peg is very pale.*]

Garrick

So, madam, you have lied to me!

Peg

Yes.

Garrick

It was his wig?

Peg

Yes.

Garrick

Pish! Macklin was right. As well expect constancy in a—

Peg

Stop! David, if you refuse to listen to me now you will repent it all your life!

Garrick

Listen to you? I shall repent all my life that I ever did!

LOVELY PEGGY

Peg

Then from this very hour we separate! Had you been worthy to hear the truth, I would have told it to you, but it is ended for ever! To think that I, Peg Woffington, still believed in honor and love!

[*Laughs unpleasantly.*]

You've opened my eyes, Mr. Garrick! Here was I, taken in by your vows like any schoolgirl,—and all the while I was nothing to you but what you could find in any green room. And I believed in it all! Good God, I believed it!

Garrick

Madam, have you the effrontery to deny your guilt in the face of this proof?

Peg

No! I admit it! I am guilty! I made an appointment here tonight with Sir Charles—we planned it well, didn't we? I knew you were going to the Bedford—Sir Charles overheard you arrange to meet your friends there,—the hour was fixed. I meant to dupe you, trick you, gull you, make a fool of you! I wanted the town to say that Peg Woffington had made a fool of David Garrick—to hear them roll it over on their tongues as they sipped their chocolate,—to see them shrug their shoulders

LOVELY PEGGY

and raise their eyebrows when you passed,—ah, you didn't know all this, did you? And you thought I cared! I've been playing with you, as I've played with dozens of others—

[*Garrick turns on his heel and strides out of the room without a word. The front door is heard to slam.*]

Peg

David! David! It isn't true! I love you!
[*She collapses in a heap on the floor.*]

QUICK CURTAIN

ACT III

SCENE: *The stage, Covent Garden. Some months later. The stage is seen from the audience as if one were standing in the wings. That is to say one is looking at it from the side. The entire right to a little beyond left-center is taken up with this reproduction of the Covent Garden stage. The candle footlights are also seen and the stage itself is lighted by many candles in a chandelier which hangs from the flies. On the left are the benches of the pit and one stage box also faces the real audience.*

The stage is set for the last act of As You Like It, and the benches in the pit are thronged with a motley crowd. All through the action on the miniature stage the audience in the pit must sustain their part in the picture.

At the rise of the real curtain, the curtain on the miniature stage is down and the applause from the pit, which is heard the moment before, dies away. The "play" audience rise and conversation among them becomes general as they pass among themselves. Ladies in extravagant costumes can be seen in the stage box. On the miniature stage, the scene-shifters are putting everything in order. John Rich is directing them.

Rich

[*Tapping with a heavy stick.*]

Blockhead! Prop up the oak tree! Would you have the Forest of Arden come tumbling about our ears?—Zounds, fellow! Don't make such an infernal row with your hammering!—The wing at the first entrance on the O. P. side is too far forward. Shift it back! Ready for the fifth act, William?

[*A general murmur in the affirmative as the scene-shifters go off. Sir Charles comes from among the audience in the pit and climbs on to the miniature stage, passing behind the curtain.*]

Sir Charles

You've a large audience, tonight, Rich.

Rich

The first in weeks. Muster Garrick is not playing at Drury Lane tonight.

Sir Charles

He's his own manager and only acts when it suits his vanity. We made a mistake, Rich, when we rejected his services.

Rich

Aye, but who could foresee that the town would go mad over him? And now I have to follow the fashions he sets—or play to empty benches!

Sir Charles

You are giving us a devilish bad performance tonight.

Rich

I know! You can't get the effects in Shakespeare that you can with a good pantomime. But the town wants Shakespeare because Muster Garrick has made him fashionable, so I let 'em have it. They flock to Drury Lane fast enough to see Hamlet and Lear, so I puts 'em on As You Like It to counteract the other house. And it hasn't paid, Sir Charles, it hasn't paid!

Sir Charles

I do not wonder at it. The Woffington is acting very badly this week.

Rich

The stubborn jade! Ah, Sir Charles, the trials of us managers! She complains of being ill! She refused to go on at all tonight at first. I told her I was too old a hand to accept that excuse. "You go on tonight as Rosalind," says I, "or I'll fine you a week's salary and give the new play to Bellamy." I heard no more about illness after that, but she's playing damned bad to spite me. She's never been the same actress since Muster Garrick would have nothing more to do with her.

Sir Charles

Turn her off, that's the best way to deal with women. They'll come back whining then.

Rich

I dare not! I've not another soul in my company can draw the town at all.

[*Tate Wilkinson, looking as poor and miserable as ever, wanders in from behind the scene on the right.*]

Sir Charles

There's the Wilkinson lad!

Rich

Aye, he's still pestering me to give him a theatrical engagement. Lord! how the fellow lives is more than I can see.

Sir Charles

[*Addressing Wilkinson.*]
Ah, Wilkinson!

Wilkinson

[*Coming forward.*]
Yes, sir?

LOVELY PEGGY

Sir Charles

What are you doing here, eh? Answer me that!

Wilkinson

I—I am hoping to secure a position, sir.

Rich

I've told ye a thousand times that ye needn't hope for anything here. I won't have you!

Wilkinson

[*Sadly.*]
I know, sir. But something might turn up,—if another actor were taken ill, for example?

Rich

I'd as soon put on one of my scene-shifters. Didn't ye disgrace my theatre once?

Wilkinson

Nevertheless, I think I'll stay.

Sir Charles

[*Suddenly bursting into laughter.*]
By Jove, I believe the fellow is in love!

Rich

You're a wag, Sir Charles! The boy's a poor penniless devil.

LOVELY PEGGY

Sir Charles

[*Still laughing.*]

I'll wager you, Rich, he's in love with the Woffington.

Wilkinson

[*Suddenly flaring up.*]

Well, sir, and if I am? I am not ashamed to own it. My love, at least, can never harm her.

Rich

Why, you fool, the woman hates and scorns you! If it had not been for her, I would have given you something to do long ago, if only to be rid of your mournful moping. But Mrs. Woffington will not have you in the theatre.

Wilkinson

I—I offended her once—without intention—and she will not forgive me. It is not her fault—I—I lack the courage to explain to her,—and I love her for it all the more.

Sir Charles

Damme, an odd fish, Rich!

[*A noise of chattering and laughter is heard off right. Enter Peg Woffington, in doublet and hose, costumed as Rosalind in the Forest of Arden. A swarm of gallants and admirers follow at her heels. Her gaiety*

LOVELY PEGGY

sounds forced and unnatural. Rich and Sir Charles go up stage. Wilkinson slinks into the shadow of one of the wings and stands watching her with hungry eyes.]

First Gallant

[*Offering a jeweled brooch.*]

Queen of my heart, will you still refuse this trinket?

Peg

[*With a mock Irish brogue.*]

Get along with yez,—palaverin' at a poor girl like me.

[*First gallant falls back discomfited. The others laugh.*]

Second Gallant

[*Offering flowers.*]

Will you teach me to make love as you teach Orlando?

Peg

Monsieur Le Beau, I take no pupils unless they have had some experience!

[*Renewed laughter by the others.*]

Third Gallant

[*Offering verses.*]

Read these verses, divinity! I would hang them on an oak tree, only there is none in London.

LOVELY PEGGY

Peg

Keep them and read them to me seven years hence. That advice is from another poet—Horace.

[*Sir Charles comes down stage to her and bows with a flourish. Peg recoils and then recovers herself. The other gallants go up stage, with bows, leaving them alone.*]

Peg

Do you have the presumption to address me, sir?

Sir Charles
[*Taking snuff.*]
Pardon me, I was not aware that I spoke first!

Peg

No matter. Your presence is an insult.

Sir Charles

It is mere common politeness, I assure you. I came to congratulate you upon getting rid of your play-actor admirer, Master Davy. 'Faith, Peg, I laugh to think how you packed him off to Drury Lane by himself. It was clever of you, Peg,—infernally clever!

Peg

Mr. Garrick has always been free to make his own plans.

Sir Charles

And now that he has made his exit,—I hope it was a graceful one, Peg?—allow me to return this keepsake which you once bestowed, reluctantly I'll admit, upon me.

[*He offers her the miniature and chain which he took from her in the last act.*]

Peg

You have carried your pleasantry far enough.

Sir Charles

Good! I am rejoiced to hear you call it that! And now that you have seen the truth at last, permit me to make amends for the past.

Peg

What do you mean?

Sir Charles

Why, look you, Peg, when I heard of Mr. Garrick's dismissal from your favor, I altered my plans. I've bought a little villa in the country,—in a quiet spot,—it's in a veritable Forest of Arden, Peggy,—and there we may live like some shepherd and shepherdess, eh?

Peg

Am I to understand that you are serious?

LOVELY PEGGY

Sir Charles

For once, I am! I offer you devotion—peace—and everything that money can buy besides. You cannot live without a protector. And with Garrick out of the way, who else but me?

Peg

[*With a frigid manner.*]

Sir, you are vastly mistaken in your ideas.

[*Turns her back on him and walks away.*]

Sir Charles

Hark'ee, Peg, not so fast! I came prepared for this too! I shall not endure any more trifling from you.

Peg

[*Turns, angry.*]

Do you dare to threaten me?

Sir Charles

It is not a threat. But if you are unreasonable, I have a remedy for that.

Peg

Well, sir, I choose to be unreasonable, as you call it. Pray have you any further business with me?

Sir Charles

Yes. If you reject this proposal, I fear very

LOVELY PEGGY

much that you will find the last act of As You Like It tonight very far from being as you like it. The pit and galleries are filled with my men,—which, by the way, accounts for friend Rich's full house. Either you consent to listen favorably to me, or the famous Mrs. Woffington will be publicly disgraced and hissed off the stage of Covent Garden!

Peg

[*Her eyes blazing.*]

If you venture to interrupt my acting with your hired bullies, the town will stone you to death! I have more friends than you think!

Sir Charles

We will see! You refuse to consent?

Peg

I have already answered you.

Sir Charles

As you wish.
[*Turns to Rich, up stage.*]
Rich! Rich! One moment, if you please.

Rich

[*Comes down stage obsequiously.*]
Your servant, Sir Charles!

Sir Charles

Rich, I have made a certain proposal to Mrs. Woffington which she has seen fit to reject. I regret that this circumstance compels me to have her hissed off the stage tonight. But I must teach her pride a lesson.

Rich

[*Whimpering with anxiety.*]
For God's sake, Sir Charles, I'll be ruined!

Sir Charles

Then use you influence with the lady.

[*Walks coolly up stage.*]

Rich

[*Imploring Peg.*]

Madam, you've heard him! You must pacify him at any cost! I'll increase your salary,— I'll do anything! With Garrick carrying all before him at Drury Lane,—it would mean ruin for us all, if you were hissed here!

Peg

[*With composure.*]

Pray, do not be uneasy, Mr. Rich. Sir Charles is not as powerful as he believes. They would not dare to hiss me! I never disappointed an audience in my life! Nor have I ever refused to play for others' benefits. Did you not hear the applause at my first entrance tonight?

LOVELY PEGGY

What reason have they to hiss me? I do not think so little of the public's gratitude as you do, Mr. Rich.

Rich

But I tell you Sir Charles may do anything! He moulds the opinion of the pit. If he pronounces against a play, nothing can save it.

Peg

I am firm in my refusal to conciliate such a man in any way. Trust the public to me, I'll manage them better than Sir Charles.

[*The call-boy shouts the summons for the fifth act. Sir Charles returns from up stage.*]

Sir Charles

Which is it to be, Mrs. Woffington, war or peace?

Peg

War!

Sir Charles

As you please.
[*Bows.*]

Rich

Sir Charles, in Heaven's name have pity on me! It means thousands of pounds to me and I'm a poor man!

LOVELY PEGGY

Peg

It means more than that to me, Mr. Rich, but I am not afraid.

Rich

It's utter ruin for us both! Sir Charles—

Sir Charles

You cringing old simpleton!

[*He walks to the curtain, pushes it to one side and passes into the pit, where way is respectfully made for him. As he takes his seat he passes a note to a man near him who goes out with it, left. On the miniature stage, the gallants gather at the wings, waiting for the act to begin. An actor and actress as Touchstone and Audrey respectively, take their places ready to go on when the curtain rises. Peg stands by one of the wings to wait for her cue. Near her stands Wilkinson.*]

Wilkinson

[*Advancing timidly.*]

Madam, I could not fail to overhear what just passed. I heard Sir Charles threaten you. If any service I could render you would prove acceptable, pray command me!

Peg

[*She is nervous.*]

Sir, the only service you can render me is to take your leave.

Wilkinson

Madam, I beg of you to listen to me for an instant! You are mistaken if you think that I ever mocked your acting! Believe me when I say that I entertain for you nothing but feelings of the most profound respect and admiration!

Peg

[*Acknowledges the statement coldly.*]

Your frank acknowledgment of your error does you credit.

[*She turns her back on him and he drops back crestfallen. David Garrick enters from the right, at this point. He comes to the center.*]

Peg

[*Starting as she sees Garrick.*]

David!

Garrick

[*Bowing.*]

Madam—I—I wish a few words with you, if I may claim the honor?

LOVELY PEGGY

Peg

[*Freezing up again.*]

Pray proceed. The act is just beginning.

[*The miniature curtain rises and the fifth act of As You Like It begins, in dumb show, with the scene between Touchstone and Audrey. There is a slight ripple of applause from the pit, but no disturbance. They are waiting for Peg Woffington's entrance. The character of William in As You Like It enters, and stands waiting in the wings for his cue. The prompter, who also stands in the wings, is seen occasionally to gesticulate violently at the characters on the miniature stage.*]

Garrick

I regret sincerely, madam, that our quarrel has had the result of making the relations between us strained.

Peg

Surely you have not come here at this time to tell me that!

Garrick

On the contrary it is the sole object of my visit. But I feel, in spite of the long friendship which once existed between us, that some apology for my presence is necessary.

LOVELY PEGGY

Peg

You need give yourself no further concern. The incident to which you refer has escaped my memory.

Garrick

[*Ironically.*]

I rejoice that it has not disturbed you in any way.

Peg

Why should it? Your conduct was only what was to be expected from a man. Friendship, as you call it, between a man and a woman is only another name for indifference.

Garrick

You have no regrets, Peg, none?

Peg

Is that a fair question? I have already informed you that the episode is erased from my memory.

Garrick

It is more than I had dared to hope! I may then discuss with you the matter of business which brings me here tonight?

Peg

Please do not longer delay it, as I expect my cue very shortly.

Garrick

As you know, my managership of Drury Lane Theatre has met with extraordinary success. Not only have I established beyond question my own reputation as the greatest living actor, but I have become even more famous for the restoration of Shakespeare to our modern stage.

Peg

Sir, if you desire to finish before my cue—

Garrick

I have always regretted that our quarrel prevented me from availing myself of your valuable services as an actress. Now that has been forgotten I conceived it would not be indelicate for you to enrol yourself in my company at Drury Lane. You would be at liberty to play those parts in which you are most famous, such as Sir Harry Wildair—

Peg

Mr. Garrick, this is the second offer to which I have listened tonight. The first one, although of a different character, was no less insulting than yours—

Garrick

Insulting?

LOVELY PEGGY

Peg

Surely, if you had any spark of manhood or decency alive in you, you would realize the impossibility of what you suggest!

Garrick

Allow me to remind you that the offer is simply a business one. My approaching marriage with Mademoiselle Violette prevents me from making a proposal of another nature.

Peg

[*Catching hold of the scenery for support.*]
Your marriage?

Garrick

Yes. The affair has only recently been arranged.

Peg

[*Her anger blazing out suddenly.*]
And yet you come here to fling your insults and your marriage in my face! Of all the despicable, petty creatures on God's earth there is none meaner and more loathsome than you! The only excuse which you have is that your vanity and self-conceit have blinded you to everything else. Never dare, as long as either of us shall live, to address another word to me on any pretext whatsoever! I have heard enough of Mr. David Garrick and his affairs!

[*As she finishes the above speech, she dashes on to the miniature scene to take her cue. Garrick stands a second as if stunned and then slinks away.*]

Peg

[*As Rosalind—gaily.*]
"God save you, brother."

[*At these words Sir Charles rises in the pit and gives a signal. Instantly the theatre is in an uproar. There are numerous cries of "Off! Off!" and men jump upon the benches. Hoots, hisses and catcalls are heard and the noise is deafening. Peg stands fearlessly, trying to quell the turmoil. Rich dashes on to the stage and is greeted with jeers. Macklin as Jacques and Quin as Duke Senior, also appear from behind the scenes and go to Peg's assistance. Wilkinson places himself quietly behind her. Several of the gallants, who have been standing in the wings, draw their swords and come on to the stage. Renewed hisses greet their appearance. The audience begin to tear up the benches, while fights and scuffles are numerous in the pit. Various objects are thrown on the stage from the galleries. The sound of broken glass is heard, as the mob smashes the mirrors around the walls. Cries of "Fire the*

LOVELY PEGGY

*house!" "Down with Woffington!" "Off!
Off!" become more frequent and violent.
The mob, led by Sir Charles, begin to climb
upon the stage. They easily beat back the
gallants with sticks and cudgels. Peg
alone stands her ground, with Wilkinson,
who does not desert her. Up stage, in one
corner, there is some sword play going on.
The mob surges about Peg. Suddenly her
voice is heard above the din.]*

Peg

[*Imperiously.*]

Back to your benches! Stop! I'll leave the stage, since you wish it!

[*An ugly shout. They fall back from her a little.*]

I'll not stay to be a mark for your spite! But I'm not afraid of you—no, nor of ten thousand devils—let alone such curs as you—and you—and you!

[*Snaps her fingers in the faces of those nearest her. They fall back before her.*]

Have I ever disappointed you?

[*A shout. Some voices, "No!"*]

You're not all hired ruffians, I see! Have I not always served you? Have I ever failed to appear when my name was billed,—whether well or ill?

LOVELY PEGGY

[*More shouts and clamor.*]

Night after night I've played for you,—it didn't matter what I felt here—

[*Touches her bosom.*]

I made *you* laugh just the same! Is this your gratitude? Is this the way you reward the public's faithful servant? For years I've humored your whims and caprices without a murmur,—played what you demanded without a question. And now you show your courage—

[*Clamor.*]

your bravery—

[*Uproar.*]

by attacking a defenceless woman! What do you want?

[*Cries of "Off! Off!"*]

What would you have me do? Do you know yourselves?

[*Renewed cries of "Off! Off!" groans and hoots.*]

So be it then! You are the judges. It shall be on or off, just as you please. It is a matter of indifference to me!

[*Cries of "Off!" are now mingled with cries of "On!"*]

I'll wait patiently for you to settle this among yourselves. I wish to know if all my years of work for you are to meet with this reward!

Sir Charles

[*Addressing the mob.*]

Will you permit the Irish jade to blarney you?

[*Cries of "No!"*]

Then it's off, off! I say!

[*Cheers and shouts and renewed fighting in the pit.*]

Peg

[*Pointing at Sir Charles.*]

If you want to know what this all means—ask him! There's the man who can tell you! He talks about Irish blarney,—but I appeal to you for British fair play!

[*Clamor and struggles.*]

Because I resented an insult at his hands tonight, he takes this revenge!

Sir Charles

It's a lie! Off! Off! The woman's a brazen hussy!

Peg

[*Strides up to Sir Charles and strikes him in the face.*]

LOVELY PEGGY

Take that lie back again!

[*A wild cheer of delight at this and shouts of "Fair play!" Sir Charles trembling with rage lifts his fists against her, but Wilkinson slips by quickly and suddenly seizing him, struggles with him to the edge of the stage where he throws him heavily into the pit. Cheer upon cheer follow this act. Cries of "Peg Woffington!" "Woffington forever!" "On! On!" Others fight their way to the front and attack Sir Charles and his party, thrusting them back. The stage is cleared after a rough and tumble tumult. Peg Woffington lays one hand on Wilkinson's arm and he stoops and reverently kisses her hand.*]

Peg

[*Raises her hand. The storm ceases as if by magic.*]

My friends!

[*A cheer which echoes and re-echoes.*]

Will you take me back?

[*Another roar of approval.*]

Then we'll end it all with an epilogue! For 'faith I think you've made Jacques so melancholy tonight he'll never speak again! and as for Orlando, I dare wager he's gone home.

LOVELY PEGGY

> [*Looks around at the empty stage behind her. Wilkinson once more stands behind the scenery in the wings.*]

If my costume does not fit the epilogue, it is because you gave me little chance to change.

> [*Laughter.*]

Will you listen to it as I am?

> [*The applause echoes again.*]

That's the music I love best!

Peg

> [*Begins at this point the epilogue of As You Like It.*]

It is not the fashion to see the lady the epilogue, but it is no more unhandsome than to see the lord the prologue. If it be true that good wine needs no bush, 'tis true that a good play needs no epilogue; yet to good wine they do use good bushes, and good plays prove the better by the help of good epilogues. What a case am I in then, that am neither a good epilogue nor can not insinuate with you in the behalf of a good play! I am not furnished like a beggar, therefore, to beg will not become me; my way is to conjure you, and I'll begin with the women. I charge you, O women, for the love you bear to men, to like as much of this play as please you; and I charge you, O men, for the love you bear to women,—as I perceive by your simpering that none of you hates them,—that between you and the women the play may please. If I were a woman I would kiss as many of you as had beards that pleased me—

[*She begins the above speech briskly but falters several times as it progresses. At the last words quoted, she staggers and falls with a cry. The audience in the pit rise in their excitement. Wilkinson rushes to her, takes her up in his arms and carries her to the wings. Bellamy as Celia, Quin, Macklin and Rich, who have reappeared from behind the scenes right, while the epilogue was being spoken, now crowd around her. The miniature curtain is hastily lowered upon a gruff order from Rich, and the audience in the pit sit in awed silence.*]

Wilkinson

Stand back—give her air! Let a physician be summoned!

[*Bends over her and raises her head.*]

I love you, Peggy!

[*The others look at one another in astonishment.*]

Peg

[*Opens her eyes and smiles faintly when she sees who it is who whispered to her.*]

I understand—I understand! I too have known what it means to be scorned by the being I loved! Forgive me!

[*She raises herself up partly with Wilkinson's assistance. He kisses her hand passionately.*]

Peg

Bellamy, child!

[*Bellamy goes to her and kneels by her weeping.*]

Bellamy

I—I am sorry for all the past!

Peg

[*Caressing her.*]

And I, I might have been kinder to you, child—but there, it's over now.

Peg

[*To the others.*]

My old friends,—we've acted in many a play together—and now I've been called for my last epilogue—

Macklin

No, no, Peggy! It's only a passing faintness—the riot—the excitement—

LOVELY PEGGY

Peg

[*Shakes her head.*]

Macklin—I know—I've only the tag left to speak. There's one favor I want to ask—before the curtain falls.

Macklin

What is it, dear?

Peg

You'll tell him how it happened, won't you?

[*Macklin much moved turns away his head.*]

I want him to know.

[*Macklin wipes his eyes and Peg seizes his hand.*]

Ah, old friend, it is better to go this way—with the last echoes of the applause in my ears! It is better than ever I dared hope!

[*She sinks back in Wilkinson's arms dead, as Garrick hurries in from the right. They make a warning gesture at him and he pauses in silence. Quin strides before the miniature curtain and raises his hand for silence as he faces the pit.*]

Quin

[*Addressing the audience in the pit.*]

Mrs. Woffington is dead!

LOVELY PEGGY

[*Silently as if awe-struck, the audience file out of the pit. Wilkinson holds the dead body in his arms. Garrick kneels at her feet.*]

SLOW CURTAIN

THE END

NOTES ON ACT I

These notes are intended merely to indicate the principal sources of some of the incidents and anecdotes made use of in this play. Wherever possible, I have chosen a historical episode, or scrap of dialogue, in preference to a fictitious one.

October, 1741: the year and month in which Garrick made his first London appearance at Goodman's Field's Theatre. This was also the year of Peg Woffington's first metropolitan success.—*Covent Garden Theatre:* built by John Rich in 1731. —*The Constant Couple:* a comedy by George Farquhar, b. 1678, d. 1707. First acted at Drury Lane in 1699. Peg Woffington played the part of Sir Harry Wildair, the leading male character in this comedy, for the first time in 1740. For a description of her acting in this part, see Macklin, p. 125.—*James Quin:* b. 1693, d. 1766. An actor of the old school and an opponent of Garrick and the new, or naturalistic, school of acting.—*George Anne Bellamy:* b. circa 1731, d. 1788. She was only ten years old at the time this play opens, but, as she was a rival of Mrs. Woffington's in later years, it has been thought permissible, for dramatic purposes, to introduce her as a well-known actress at this period. Her memoirs are the source of much of the material used in this play.—*Quin's acting:* see Davies, v. 1, p. 28; Wilkinson, v. 4, p. 79; J. Galt, v. 1, p. 184 and p. 197.— *Quin's character:* Wilkinson, v. 1, p. 186; Murphy, v. 1, p. 87.—*An impudent Irish faced girl:* the phrase was used by Conway in a letter to Horace Walpole referring to Mrs. Woffington. (See Horace Walpole: Letters to Sir Horace Mann.)—*Robert Wilks:* b. 1665? d. 1732. Created the part of Sir Harry Wildair. Farquhar attributed the success of his play to Wilks' acting.—*Mrs. Woffington's voice:* see Wilkinson, v. 1,

p. 25. Also referred to by Bellamy, Lewes, and Macklin in their memoirs.—*Quin's grand pause:* see Davies, p. 106. It was really Macklin who was most famous for a "grand pause," and it was he who once knocked a prompter down for interrupting it.—*Sir Charles Hanbury Williams:* b. 1709, d. 1759. Famous for his wit and gallantries. He wrote numerous verses to Peg Woffington. These poems are printed in his complete works.—*The Bedford Coffee House:* a famous meeting place for the critics, wits, and literary men of the day. It stood in Covent Garden.—*Quin's advice:* see J. Galt, v. 1, p. 194.—*John Rich:* b. 1692, d. 1761. He was the first manager to introduce pantomime into England and was a noted Harlequin. He was responsible for Mrs. Woffington's London début. See Wilkinson for many amusing anecdotes of Rich.—*Thomas Betterton:* b. 1635? d. 1710. The famous actor of the Restoration.—*Rich as Richard III.:* Rich, who was an uneducated man with a raucous voice, was particularly fond of boasting of his ability in this part.—*Rich and his quarrels with his actors:* see Davies, v. 1, p. 135.—*Ipswich:* Garrick made his first appearance on any stage in this town during the summer of 1741.—*Garrick's rejection by Rich:* see Murphy, v. 1, p. 20; Bio. Dram., v. 1, p. 261.—*Garrick and his three quarts of vinegar:* this epigram on the calling followed by Garrick before he became an actor was made by Foote.—*Quin's gruffness:* see Wilkinson, v. 1, p. 33; Bellamy, v. 1, p. 62.—*"The Orphan":* by Thomas Otway, b. 1651, d. 1685. First acted 1680. Monimia was the chief female character. Her woes have made the part proverbial as a type of suffering innocence. This play was much admired by Dr. Johnson.—*Rich's treatment of manuscripts:* see J. Galt, v. 1, p. 193; Molloy's L. of W., v. 1, p. 76.—*Bellamy's rivalry of Mrs. Woffington:* see the memoirs of Bellamy, Macklin, and Wilkinson

LOVELY PEGGY

for details of these greenroom squabbles.—*The description of Mrs. Woffington:* see Wilkinson, v. 1, pp. 120-121; J. Galt, v. 1, p. 221.—*Cox's Museum:* a favorite resort where mechanical wonders were exhibited. References to this museum occur in Fanny Burney's "Evelina" and Sheridan's "The Rivals."—*An orange woman:* this reference is to an episode in Mrs Woffington's early life when she sold oranges in the streets of Dublin. Foote burlesqued her at the Haymarket as an orange woman to a playhouse.—*Tate Wilkinson:* b. 1739, d. 1803. His own memoirs contain the best account of his life. His application to Rich for a position on the stage, and Mrs. Woffington's scorn of him, for a real or imagined slight, are most graphically told in the pages of his reminiscences. It will be noted that his introduction is another anticipation of historical chronology.—*Charles Macklin:* b. 1697? d. 1797. His memoirs, by Cooke, are an interesting but somewhat unreliable biography. Lewes' memoirs contain descriptions of his person and manners. I have modified the harshness of his character in order to contrast him with Quin. He and Quin were rivals and once quarreled bitterly, although in public they maintained an armed neutrality toward one another. The anecdote of posterity and the condemnation of Macklin's play is from J. Galt, v. 1, p. 199.—*Quin's retort to Woffington:* this piece of repartee appears, with variations, in nearly all the theatrical memoirs of the period.—*Garrick's first meeting with Peg Woffiington:* the exact date is uncertain, but it is probable that he first became acquainted with her at the beginning of, or just before, the season of 1741-42. In the summer of 1742 he journeyed to Dublin with her, where they played at Smock Alley Theatre until time to return for the opening of the London season. (See Davies and Murphy and the contemporary memoirs.)—*Oroonoko:* by Thomas

LOVELY PEGGY

Southerne, b. 1660, d. 1746. A dramatization of Mrs. Aphra Behn's novel, "The History of Oroonoko." The play was first acted in 1696. The part of Aboan, a slave, is a secondary one, but offers a good opportunity to the actor.—*The Rival Queens:* by Nathaniel Lee, b. 1653? d. 1692. The play was first acted in 1677.—*Lothario:* the principal male character in Nicholas Rowe's (b. 1673, d. 1718) "The Fair Penitent." The character is that of a libertine and seducer. The play was first acted in 1703.—*The inserted speeches:* these are altered, for the purposes of this scene, from "The Rival Queens," v. 1. Statira and Roxana were the names of the two rival queens contending for Alexander's hand.—*Macklin's encouragement of Garrick's acting:* see Macklin, p. 97.—*Goodman's Field's Theatre:* built in 1729 and pulled down in 1746. Giffard was manager of it.—*The verses to Mrs. Woffington:* these appear in the Gentleman's Magazine, entitled "To Sylvia," and were signed D. G. They have also been ascribed to Sir Charles Hanbury Williams. Prof. George Pierce Baker, of Harvard, has reprinted them in his "Some Unpublished Correspondence of David Garrick." The latter version has an additional stanza not found in the other copies.—*Pity's akin to love:* a quotation from Southerne's "Oroonoko."—*Garrick's opinion of Mrs. Woffington's Sir Harry Wildair:* see Dutton Cook, v. 1, ch. xii.—*The Recruiting Officer:* Farquhar's most successful comedy. It was first acted at Drury Lane in 1706. The part of Sylvia is the principal female character.

NOTES ON ACT II

Domestic arrangements in Southampton Street: see Macklin, p. 118; Knight, pp. 54 and 57.—*The Daily Post and The Champion:* these quotations are from criticisms of Garrick's first London appearance as Richard III. The notice in the *Champion* was written by Fielding.—*A dozen dukes:* Knight, p. 42.—*Garrick's acting and its effect upon the stage:* among innumerable references to this, see particularly Lewes, v. 2, p. 110; Horace Walpole, Letter to Sir Horace Mann, May 26, 1742, and Murphy and Davies, Garrick's biographers.—*The ring episode:* Murphy, v. 1, p. 17.—*Garrick's avarice:* the defenders of Garrick's character maintain that his reputation for avarice is undeserved. They assure us that, like the mythical Scot, Garrick was merely careful with his money. On the other hand, the tradition of his parsimony is so often repeated that I have not hesitated to make dramatic use of the legend. See also Davies, v. 2, pp. 394-5; Murphy, v. 2, p. 194; Macklin, p. 144; Boswell, v. 2, pp. 270-1; *ibid.,* v. 2, p. 412; *ibid.,* v. 3, pp. 48-9.—*The diamond shoe buckles:* Macklin, p. 121.—*Not for an age:* Molloy's L. of W., v. 1, p. 135.—*Johnson's opinion of Garrick:* Boswell, v. 3, p. 98; *ibid.,* v. 2, p. 215; *ibid.,* v. 2, p. 118; *ibid.,* v. 1, p. 264; *ibid.,* v. 1, p. 422; *ibid.,* v. 2, p. 152; *ibid.,* v. 2, p. 356; *ibid.,* v. 2, p. 446; *ibid.,* v. 3, p. 268; *ibid.,* v. 2, p. 256; *ibid.,* v. 1, p. 394.—*Twopence halfpenny in your pocket:* Knight, p. 13; Boswell, v. 1, p. 54.—*Johnson gives Garrick a lesson in acting:* Boswell, v. 1, p. 103.—*Johnson in the greenroom:* Boswell, v. 1, p. 125.—*Garrick and Johnson's tragedy "Irene":* Boswell, v. 1, p. 121; Davies, v. 1, p. 11; Murphy, p. 207.—*Where the devil are your actors:* Macklin, p. 100.—*Johnson's opinion of actors:* Boswell, v. 2, p. 356; *ibid.,* v. 2, p. 172.—*Garrick's epigram on John-*

LOVELY PEGGY

son's Dictionary: Boswell, v. 1, p. 197. The dictionary was not published until 1755, hence neither the work nor the epigram was in existence at this time.—*Garrick's conversation:* Murphy, pp. 197-8.—*Macklin on critics:* Macklin, p. 74; *ibid.,* p. 139.—*Garrick's epigram on Quin:* Murphy, v. 1, pp. 31-2.—*Roscius:* the name was given to Garrick in Dublin while playing the summer engagement there with Mrs. Woffington in 1741. See Murphy, v. 1, p. 39.—*Johnson drinks tea with Garrick and Mrs. Woffington:* Boswell, v. 2, p. 413.—*The song "Lovely Peggy":* this song was included in the complete works of Hanbury Williams, published in 1822. It has also been ascribed to Garrick, particularly by Macklin, p. 116, and Joseph Knight, who reprints it entire in his Life of Garrick, p. 54.— *A Man of the Last Century:* this was Macklin's favorite description of himself.—*The wild Irishman:* an epithet often applied to Macklin. See Macklin, p. 5.— *The beautiful V.:* Mademoiselle Violette whom Garrick afterwards married.—*The guinea that went to the devil:* it was Foote who made this retort to Garrick. See Molloy's L. of W., v. 1, p. 211.—*The episode of the wig:* see Macklin, p. 116.—*The quarrel between Garrick and Mrs. Woffington:* see Macklin, p. 119; Wilkinson, v. 1, p. 33; Knight, p. 87 ff.—*Garrick's character:* Dibdin, v. 5. p. 102; Lewes, v. 2, p. 104.—*Garrick's love of fame:* Murphy, v. 2, p. 196.

NOTES ON ACT III.

Garrick's success at Drury Lane: Davies, v. 1, p. 111.
—*Garrick restores Shakespeare to the stage:* Davies, v. 1, p. 120.—*Young gallants in the wings:* one of the theatrical nuisances of the day was the presence of these worthies behind the scenes and even on the stage itself. Contemporary memoirs are full of references to the annoyance occasioned to both actors and audiences by this custom.—*Garrick's marriage:* an extraordinary but wholly untrustworthy account of this is to be found in Lewes, v. 2, p. 66. His wife was a Viennese dancer, Mademoiselle Violette.—*Theatre riots:* Mrs. Woffington once quelled a riot of a similar nature while playing in Dublin. See J. Galt, v. 1, pp. 187-190.—*Mrs. Woffington's collapse:* see Wilkinson, v. 1, p. 117.

For contemporary biographical sketches of Mrs. Woffington, see Lewes, Davies, and Macklin. John Hoole, b. 1727, d. 1803, wrote a Monody on the death of Mrs. Woffington. Of her power as an actress Macklin, Murphy, Dibdin and Wilkinson all have much to say. In addition, Charles Reade in his novel Peg Woffington, pp. 10-11, has characterized her charm and beauty in words which are almost a paraphrase of Macklin's.

BIBLIOGRAPHY

SOURCES OF LOVELY PEGGY.

The Life and Adventures of Peg Woffington, by Fitzgerald Molloy in 2 vols. London, 1884.

Peg Woffington, a Novel, by Charles Reade. London, 1895.

Memoirs of the Life of David Garrick, Esq., by Thomas Davies, 2 vols. London, 1781.

Life of David Garrick, by Arthur Murphy, 2 vols. London, 1801.

David Garrick, by Joseph Knight, F. S. A. London, 1894.

Garrick and His Circle, by Mrs. Clement Parsons. London, 1906.

The Lives of the Players, by John Galt, 2 vols. London, 1831.

Some Unpublished Correspondence of David Garrick, edited by George Pierce Baker. Boston, 1907.

Memoirs of His Own Life, by Tate Wilkinson, 4 vols. York, 1790.

Memoirs of Charles Macklin, Comedian, by William Cooke, Esq. London, 1806.

Mémoires de Mistriss Bellamy, traduit par M. Thiers. Paris, 1822.

Memoirs of Charles Lee Lewes, written by himself, 4 vols. London, 1805.

LOVELY PEGGY

The Life of Samuel Johnson, by James Boswell: Edited by Arnold Glover, with an introduction by Austin Dobson, 3 vols. London, 1901.

The Life and Times of Oliver Goldsmith, by John Forster, 2 vols. London, 1877.

Some Account of the English Stage, by Genest.

A New History of the English Stage, by Percy Fitzgerald. London, 1882.

The Romance of the English Stage, by Percy Fitzgerald. London, 1874.

Annals of the English Stage, by John Doran, 2 vols. London, 1865.

In and about Drury Lane, by Dr. John Doran, 2 vols. London, 1881.

The History of the Irish Stage, by Hitchcock.

The Romance of the Irish Stage, by J. Fitzgerald Molloy. London, 1897.

The London Stage, by H. Barton Baker. London, 1889.

Nichol's Literary Anecdotes (for anecdotes of Garrick and Woffington).

Representative Actors, by W. Clark Russell. London, 1872.

Hours with the Players, by Dutton Cook.

Actors and Actresses of Great Britain and the United States, by Brander Matthew and Lawrence Hutton, New York, 1886. (The volume entitled: Garrick and his Contemporaries.)

LOVELY PEGGY

English Actors, by H. Barton Baker, 2 vols. New York, 1879.

Letters of Horace Walpole, 9 vols. London, 1877. (A few selections only.)

Horace Walpole, A Memoir, by Austin Dobson. New York, 1892.

Eighteenth Century Vignettes, by Austin Dobson. New York, 1892.

Evelina, by Frances Burney.

A Complete History of the English Stage, by Charles Dibdin (1745-1814), 5 vols. London, 1800.

Sir Charles Hanbury Williams' Works, 3 vols. London, 1822.

Biographia Dramatica (1747-66). London, 1812.

The Dictionary of National Biography.

Masks and Faces, a comedy, by Charles Reade and Tom Taylor.

The Constant Couple, by Farquhar.

The Recruiting Officer, by Farquhar.

The Fair Penitent, by Rowe.

Alexander the Great, by Southerne.

Oroonoko, by Southerne.

The references to page and volume given in the notes refer to the above editions.

OHIO UNIVERSITY

Date Due